The problems and pitfalls of "life together" —
and how to cope with them victoriously

MARRIAGE is for LIVING

Compiled by BRUCE LARSON
and the editors of *Faith at Work*

ZONDERVAN PUBLISHING HOUSE
OF THE ZONDERVAN CORPORATION
GRAND RAPIDS, MICHIGAN 49506

MARRIAGE IS FOR LIVING
Copyright © 1968 by Zondervan Publishing House
Grand Rapids, Michigan

All rights reserved. No portion of this book
may be reproduced in any way
without the written permission of the publishers,
except for brief excerpts in reviews, etc.

Library of Congress Catalog Card Number 68-10521

First printing 1968
Second printing 1969
Third printing June 1970
Fourth printing December 1970
Fifth printing February 1971
Sixth printing September 1971
Seventh printing January 1972
Eighth printing August 1972
Ninth printing October 1972
Tenth printing 1973
Eleventh printing February 1974

NOTE: All of the stories in this book are true;
only the names of the people have been changed.
They were first printed, under the true names
of the authors in *Faith at Work* magazine.
The articles, too, first appeared in *Faith at Work,*
with the exception of those articles by
Bruce Larson, Lionel A. Whiston, and G. R. Slater,
which are printed here for the first time.

Printed in the United States of America

Contents

PROLOGUE: *What Is a "Christian" Marriage?*
by Sam Shoemaker / 11

I. OFF TO A BAD START / 21
   Giving Is Getting: A Couple Seeks Security in Each Other / 21
   Things Began to Happen: "Keeping Up With the Joneses" / 26
   Back Together: Divorce Was the "Solution" / 30
   The Christian View of Sex in Marriage, by Bruce Larson / 36

II. FOR BETTER AND FOR WORSE / 45
   Wishing on a Star: Anything to Escape Responsibility / 45
   Everything Is Different: Facing Up to the Past / 49
   When the Wine Runs Out, by G. R. Slater / 55
   Driving Without Brakes: Civic Duties and Home Neglect / 60
   Scraping the Bottom: Budget Problems Bring on Crisis / 64

III. WHEN THE JITTERS TAKE OVER / 71
   The End of the Rope: Rough Stuff — With Failure Ahead / 71
   My Screaming, Hateful Self: The Children Drove Her Wild / 75
   Why Opposites Attract, by Lionel A. Whiston / 78
   Why Me, Lord?: They Couldn't Have a Baby / 86

	A Day (Un)Like Any Other: Job Demands Get Out of Hand	/ 88
	Marriage Is Four Strands, by Walden Howard	/ 93
IV.	THAT FOURTH DIMENSION	/ 103
	A Question of Surrender: A Child Dies and Terror Reigns	/ 103
	Typical: Selfish Religion and a Breakdown in Communication	/ 107
	Out of Bitterness: Would Adoption Help Matters?	/ 110
	"This Has Me Licked!": Mother-in-Law Problems	/ 112
	"Adequate" — for What?: Discontent and the Status Quo	/ 114
	If You Want to Change the World: Focus for Idealism	/ 119
V.	CHILDREN: COMPLICATION OR COMPENSATION?	/ 127
	Glad We Get Along: Decision-Making Poses Difficulties	/ 127
	Asthma and an Answer: A Scrape with Psychosomatic Illness	/ 130
	Hurdles to Happiness, by Julie Harris	/ 132
	How Young Is Too Young?: Teaching a Child to Pray	/ 137
	Time for a Round-Table: Family Squabble Leads to Experiment	/ 140
	The Baby Is in Good Hands: Mental Retardation Strikes Home	/ 142

EPILOGUE: *Family Life and Faith,*
by Horace C. Lukens / 149

PROLOGUE

What Is a "Christian" Marriage?

by SAM SHOEMAKER[*]

Marriage is, of course, as old as the race, and from earliest times man has established customs and ceremonies in connection with it. Christianity began when "the Word was made flesh," and it has been a part of the genius of Christianity to lift and ennoble all natural things. We believe intensely in the sacramental character of marriage — as a natural thing which is transformed by the touch of God, and as one of the ways in which God makes Himself known in the world.

The marriage service carries more than the rite by which two persons are united: it carries also the Christian philosophy of marriage. It is "holy matrimony" in which they are to be joined, an "honorable estate." "Instituted of God," it signifies to us "the mystical union that is between Christ and His Church." It would be difficult to think of a higher conception of marriage than this.

The service goes on, "and therefore is not by any to be entered into unadvisedly or lightly; but reverently, discreetly, advisedly, soberly, and in the fear of God." Here is set forth the frame of mind in which marriage is to be undertaken. The three points seem to be: *seriousness*, which

---

[*]Author of *Under New Management, Extraordinary Living for Ordinary Men,* and many other books.

considers how important a step marriage is; *wisdom,* which looks all 'round the picture before taking the step; and *faith,* which acts in this great matter only with the approval and help of God.

We might, in the light of this philosophy, see what are the tests for a true marriage to be undertaken.

The first test is the mutual attraction of human love — the natural side of marriage. This attraction includes physical, intellectual, and social factors. Emotional factors are likely to be more prominent in the early stages, while social and intellectual rapport deepens with time. No marriage is complete without real human love, but no marriage long remains complete which is based only on sexual attraction. In days like ours, when the ties of marriage are so lightly broken, there is more danger that physical and emotional factors be considered the only ones that matter, and if these decline, to look upon the marriage as a failure.

The second test is the bond of common interests. Of course, differing interests enrich a marriage if there is a basic unity and loyalty, but some common concern is essential. Children may provide it, but sometimes children suffer the consequences of their parents' not having found it.

One of the wisest words on marriage I know comes from Dr. William E. Hocking of Harvard: "The only being you can love is the being who has an independent object of worship, and who holds you out of your self-indulgence to a worship of that same object." So far as I can see, there is only one "object of worship" with an equal claim upon all people, and that is God. The basic factor in loyalty to each other is loyalty to God. The one Power that can cement a relationship, giving it one common purpose, and changing differences to enrichments instead of barriers, is God. Every human relation, but especially marriage, should be, not like

What Is a "Christian" Marriage? / 13

two dots at the end of a line, but like two angles at the base of a triangle, with God as the apex.

The third test then becomes the readiness of each person to take spiritual responsibility for the other person. This implies a maturity that can come only from a real experience of God in one's own life. It requires an objectivity that is not influenced by emotional factors, nor those of self-interest, but sees the other person clearly, lovingly, and creatively. In this sense, no one is fit for marriage who is not fully adult; and no one is fully adult who is not spiritually aware.

That is why so many marriages fail today — the partners are so immature, so selfish, so unschooled in real living that they cannot take spiritual responsibility for each other or for their children. That is why the proportion of marriages that succeed between definitely religious people is vastly higher than between people who care nothing for God. God in your life means maturity. Maturity is the basis for responsibility. Willingness and the capacity to take spiritual responsibility for the other person are parts of the test of a thoroughly happy and unselfish marriage.

The fourth test of whether a marriage is intended between two people lies in whether it makes them love other people more, or love them less. Show me a love that is today so selfish it wants to feed only on itself, and share none of its happiness with others, and I will show you a marriage that will be tomorrow so selfish it will sicken of its own satiety. A really great human love does not drain off all one's affections in one direction: it increases and enhances one's love for all.

Every man and wife should be "father" and "mother" to many besides their own children, and every home should be the joy of many besides those who live in it. This kind of unselfishness should be in a relationship from the beginning; and if it is not there, it should be sought as essential to a true, lasting, happy, and creative marriage.

How, then, can we create Christian homes?

First, they must have God at the head of them. Not father or mother — important as their responsibility is; not some yammering youngster; not somebody's temper, or somebody's tears. But God the head, the deciding factor. They must be homes where God is talked about, loved, and His will sought by all. Human nature being what it is, there are bound to be clashes of temperament and differences of opinion. We do not want homes where there is so much law that there is no freedom. Neither do we want homes where there is so much freedom that there is no law.

There is but one final law and it is the law of God. Parents are subject to this as well as children. Parents get away from it as well as children do, and must be willing to admit it to each other and to their children. When an issue arises, instead of hot tempers and shrill voices, let us get onto our knees and ask God what *He* wants. We need steady provision for our personal prayers, and then at some time in the day for family prayers, as well. Husbands and wives should begin their married life with daily prayers together.

Second, we need homes that are characterized by homely virtues. Thrift needs to come into many homes: not niggardliness, but economy which will make more generosity possible, using all of everything. Hospitality must be there: open hearts and open doors; not a selfish retiring into our own privacy all the time, but a sharing of food and friendship with others.

Responsibility is needed: everyone with some home duties which he fulfills, which gets the work done and makes

What Is a "Christian" Marriage? / 15

all feel needed and useful. Honesty is essential: honesty about money, and about deeper feelings. Consideration we must have: remembering that everyone's plans and interests are important to him, and helping him to fulfill them unselfishly.

Self-giving there must be: paying attention to others, taking an interest in what interests them, giving them time. And we need plenty of good play between young and old.

Third, Christian homes must be homes where people are growing spiritually. When two people settle down to be what Chesterton calls "their own petty little selves," it becomes about as exciting as for two bricks to settle down beside each other in a wall. Unless you have a spiritual motivation, unless God is in your life, working with you, helping you to grow, you become an unutterable bore, a continuous repetition of yourself.

When no one in the family can get after you for your moods or your habits, when you have fenced yourself off from correctives from God and the people nearest you, you are dead inside and might as well be dead outside. Only God keeps people growing. And only growing, being more and more different from our old selfish selves, keeps us from being impossible to live with.

Fourth, they should be homes where other people find new life and spirit. If two people, and their children, are under God, there will be something attractive and creative about the home in which they live. When God is present there is no missing Him. Surely He wants to use the homes He has blessed, that other homes may be blessed through them.

Many homes are without God. Let us pray that the contagion of Christian homes may pass over to those that are darker because they lack God. There is something definitely sacramental, "an outward and visible sign of an inward and spiritual grace," about a really Christian marriage, and the spirit of it becomes contagious.

* * *

Having taken this cursory look at some aspects of what might be called a "Christian" marriage, let us see how one young couple got started in such a relationship.

We shall call him "Jim" and his wife "Mary," though these are not their names. I met them when they were planning to be married. I also knew Jim's brother and his wife, and all four were attractive, capable people, able to hold up their end in this world.

I was drawn to Jim and Mary. They asked me to advise them about some things, and we became friends. Later they began coming to church once in a while, and my wife and I invited them to a couples' group which met on Sunday evenings where we talked informally about Christ and the relevance of religion today. They knew very little and asked elementary questions, but with increased knowledge and continued exposure, they became more interested and began to attend regularly. They started to read their Bible at home, and came to church fairly regularly. They were increasingly open to the whole Christian claim on them.

One day Jim said, "My wife and I want to make our full Christian decision, and we think now would be a good time to do it. Can we get together after one of the services?" I said, "Of course," and the three of us went into the chapel and knelt at the altar rail.

After a short time, Jim began to pray aloud, saying something like this: "Dear God, this is Mary and Jim and Sam.

What Is a "Christian" Marriage?   / 17

Mary and I are strangers to You. We want to come in now and be a part of Your big family, and we hope You will take us in." Then Mary said a prayer as simple and moving as her husband's, and I prayed for them.

Afterward Jim asked if they might make their communion next day, and I thought this was right. I wish you could have seen their profound joy as they knelt at the communion rail. It was a day of complete dedication to Christ.

A couple of weeks later I talked with Jim about his next steps. He and Mary were both keeping regular times for prayer and Bible study in the morning, and they were coming steadily to church. I asked how this was working out in daily contacts. He told me that they had taken God fully into partnership in their business, and were asking Him for guidance, and felt they had never done such good work. Moreover their friends had noticed such a change in them that they remarked on it. He said, "I failed this week to tell one person who asked me what it was, I just flunked it; but I have talked with several more and they are greatly interested. We just tell them honestly what has happened and what Christ is doing for us."

I then asked him whether he had yet surrendered his bank account to God, and he said, "Not altogether — what do you think we ought to do about that?" I said that I had for years tithed, giving at least one tenth of my income to God's direct work, and that most people who did this found it a blessing.

We said no more then; two weeks later my wife and I were having dinner with them, and Jim said, "Mary and I have thought over what you said. We are going to tithe, too."

Think of it — young Christians, new to this life, yet already tithing their income, and witnessing gladly to their friends about what Christ had done for them. A few thousand couples like that could lift the level of this nation. Will you and the person to whom you are married begin? Yours can be as dynamic and wonderful an experience as Jim's and Mary's has been.

I. Off to a Bad Start

I. Off to a Bad Start

Giving Is Getting

Arnold and Peggy were from the right side of the tracks, and had the advantages of a good education and an adequate income — but these factors didn't solve their problem when they discovered they had married for "all the wrong reasons." Faith at Work Editor Walden Howard tells their story.

The little house across from the golf course seemed tranquil inside and out when I stopped by on a Sunday afternoon to meet Arnold and Peggy Thompson. Arnold was toying with his new tape recorder. Peggy was washing dishes, but tossed off her apron and joined us in the living room.

"It doesn't seem real for us to be together and so happy," they began, and unfolded the tale of a marriage that four Januarys ago was dying but now obviously is a thriving romance.

They had met in college back in Ohio, and their marriage was uneventful, except for little Cynthia who came crippled with cerebral palsy and tied Peggy down to the house. They moved to the East and were doing well — to all outward appearances — but inwardly they were becoming increasingly unhappy. Peggy blamed it on being confined with Cynthia, and on Arnold, who was coming home later and drinking more and dodging his responsibilities. Arnold blamed it on Peggy. And so both of them began pulling away, resenting each other and withdrawing from their marriage in patterns that were well established from childhood.

Peggy, an only child whose parents were divorced when she was seven, had never known the security of a normal family. She came home after school, let herself in (because Mother was working), got an apple, roller-skated awhile, did her homework, and went to bed. Mother had "put the fear of God into her," however, and it kept Peggy in line, active at church and on good behavior; but she was independent and she carried this trait into marriage.

When she felt Arnold drawing away, Peggy revived her interest in singing. She'd been a voice major at college, and dreamed of herself as another Mary Martin. She longed for freedom from the restrictions of home and from her uncertainty about Arnold.

Arnold withdrew in his own way. He had started drinking at fourteen. He doesn't know why, except that boys and girls in his home town started tasting life early. His own parents seemed old-fashioned and naive in their morals, so he rebelled and broke away. "But the day I started drinking I stopped growing," Arnold says. "I began to use alcohol to solve all my problems. I drank to relax. I drank when I was sad and when I was happy."

The day came when Arnold realized Peggy wasn't the most glamorous creature in the world and perhaps he had made a mistake in marrying her and ought to go out and find another girl, and he had to drown his disappointment in drink. Then when he realized he had a responsibility to Peggy and couldn't leave her, he had to drink to face it.

All his inner conflicts responded beautifully — momentarily, at least — to alcohol. As he withdrew more and more

Off to a Bad Start / 23

into himself and his problems — and his bottle — he drifted further and further away from Peggy.

The conference at the local Methodist Church couldn't have come at a more appropriate time. Peggy went, and in a small conversational group poured out her resentment and self-pity. One of the leaders had the courage to suggest that her dreams of a singing career were her own escape hatch — like Arnold's alcohol. He asked if she had done anything to change *herself.*

Peggy listened as he spoke of a love that breeds love, that gives unconditionally, regardless of the response. For twenty-four hours she inventoried her life and found that she had *never* given that kind of love!

The next time she saw her new friend, they prayed together. He assured Peggy that God could handle her problems and show her how to face them. Peggy believed it was possible. "It was like walking a tightrope," she recalls, "but there was a net down below — I hoped — and something inside said, 'Go ahead and try it.'"

She began the experiment of putting Arnold and the girls first, submerging her own desires. In the experiment she discovered the Christian paradox: in giving you receive. The more she gave herself to God and relinquished her resentments against Arnold, the more he responded and grew as a responsible person. "It took someone to start it," she says.

I've got to give this a real try, she thought. *All I can do is to try to love as Christ would love. No matter what Arnold does, he's going to get love from me before I give up on our marriage.*

The first result was that Peggy felt happy, even when Arnold didn't come home in the evening. Occasionally she failed, but most of the time she felt herself possessed by a love beyond her own. She says, "I experienced the Holy Spirit."

Did she become less of a person herself — a doormat? Just the opposite. "I felt for the first time like a woman, able to put the man in my home first," she explains. No longer was she playing mother to a little boy and wanting to run away from it all. She was staying where she was and living as she should. And the more she put Arnold first, the more he changed and carried his share of the load.

Arnold was amazed by Peggy's new behavior. He knew it was something she wasn't capable of — like the very special morning he lay in bed with a hangover and Peggy, instead of "chewing him out," tenderly massaged his back.

She didn't talk about what had happened, but he knew something had. He also knew that she met with a small group down the street, and he teased her about her "crying sessions." But he was happy to have the pressure off. He could drink now as he pleased — and perhaps, too, there was something in all this for him.

A year after Peggy began her experiment, she persuaded Arnold to go with her to a church retreat. He was scared and miserable, but again it couldn't have come at a more opportune time. He was just getting over a binge and feeling sorry for himself — sorry enough to weep in his talk-it-over group, feeling like an utter fool but unable to stop.

Out of the diminishing fog of the drinking spree and the retreat, Arnold was left with one strong desire. He wanted to go to church. The following Sunday he had a date with a customer in New York to watch the Giants play football. As he drove down the turnpike he tuned the radio to a church service, and the desire to get inside a church flooded over him.

He turned off the turnpike at the next town and sure

Off to a Bad Start / 25

enough, there was a big white frame church. *But what if there are people in there and they ask me what I'm doing?* he thought.

Silencing his fears, he obeyed his first impulse and went in. The sanctuary was empty except for the organist who was rehearsing with his back to the door. Arnold slipped into a pew, dropped to his knees, and wept. He asked God to take over his life. It was a vaguely comprehended commitment because he had never believed in God. The very idea of God had seemed illogical to him, and he had jumped at any chance to argue about it with a clergyman.

But now he started going to church regularly and trying to keep sober. He told himself he could solve his drinking problem privately and not have to go to "that awful group, Alcoholics Anonymous." After a year of attending church and still getting drunk and having the minister drop by at all the wrong times, he swallowed his pride, went to AA, and got sober. Arnold now goes to AA meetings every week because he needs to be reminded that just one drink can undo the last two years of sobriety.

God has come into focus for Arnold. When he wanted to join the church, he could not swallow the divinity of Jesus Christ and the idea of the Trinity. Some of the men in the church invited him on a hunting trip to Canada in October. "They were crazy people," Arnold says. "They hunted and sang hymns and prayed and read the Bible." They didn't argue with him but gave him a Bible to read. When he came back to the membership class at church, he was able to say, "I believe."

In the months that followed, Arnold discovered Peggy's secret for himself: "In giving your life to the Lord He gives it back to you a hundredfold. You can stop worrying about your problems because the Lord is taking care of them.

Then you can become a person. You can get out of your own way and love other people."

Are all their problems solved? No, there's still an occasional argument. Arnold will see a towel on the rug as he leaves for work. Annoyance will begin to fester. Soon he's resenting Peggy. When he comes home, he's forgotten what caused it, but she can sense his anger and soon they're arguing without even knowing why.

Then one of them has to start "the experiment" — whoever thinks of it first and is willing to say, "I'm sorry." As they talk it over and pray, the resentment vanishes and love flows freely once more.

Things Began to Happen

Burt and Sandra found that their ambitions, once achieved, turned to ashes, and they became weighed down with the aimlessness and futility of "keeping up with the Joneses." Then a thirty-day experiment revolutionized their marriage.

What kind of life can a man and woman build for themselves and their family while ignoring God? This was the central problem for my wife and me, yet we were completely unaware of it.

I was a steadily rising "young executive," the head of a small business. We went to church irregularly, and our goals consisted of material gains and improvements. The trouble was that when achieved, these failed to give any lasting satisfaction.

Our home life was often irritable for no clear-cut reason, and our children learned early that love can be mixed with resentment, edginess, and impulsive, unloving discipline.

Off to a Bad Start / 27

This sort of existence forced us finally to seek the advice of a clergyman.

My wife and I are both "only children," and have a similar church background. We've both had college training, though my education was interrupted by war. All in all, we should have had whatever it takes to cope with life's ordinary problems, marital and otherwise.

Yet salary increases were never quite sufficient; they only whetted our appetite for more. Ambitions, once achieved, turned to ashes. Ahead of us stretched dreary years of keeping up with the Joneses. Was there any point in all this? The aimlessness and futility of such a life began to weigh us down.

One afternoon found us in a minister's study and he listened to our story, with its self-righteous acceptance of a little blame for ourselves and a lot for others. After musing for a while, he startled us by saying, "Let's pray about this," and getting down on his knees. Since there didn't seem to be any decent way out of this, we joined him. After praying aloud he matter-of-factly suggested that we do likewise, turning our problems over to God. We stumbled through petitions to a Divine Power we were not even sure existed. Then we said the Lord's Prayer, holding hands, and I was struck by the feeling that a great weight was being lifted. Somewhere within me hope stirred that we were on the right track.

The minister had asked us to pray to "as much of God as we understood." This was not difficult. Now he challenged us to give God a fair chance. If we would embark on a certain course of action for thirty days, he said, God would begin to clean up our lives and change our outlook.

We were to begin by attending a weekly class on "How To Become a Christian." Right away I felt apprehensive.

Me — a Christian? I thought Christ was a great teacher and moralist, and quite useful as a bone to throw to the children, but for adults His teachings didn't seem to fit into the rat-race of business and social life.

The second part of our "program" was to be a weekly discussion group, in which couples met to offer mutual support in the attempt to bring Christ more fully into their lives. At home we were to read a chapter of the Bible every day, pray aloud before going to bed, and spend at least fifteen minutes a day in quiet meditation, trying to keep our minds and hearts open to "God's communication."

Then things began to happen!

During the first thirty days of the program, we saw enough of a change taking place so that we were ready to throw ourselves wholeheartedly into the quest for God's guidance and purpose in our lives.

Years passed, and in time we came to feel truly happy and content. Material things no longer dominated our lives, for we saw that everything we had or were was from God. We learned to tithe and found that our money was adequate for whatever we needed.

We learned the power of prayer and have seen it work mighty things in our own and our friends' lives. God has proved His love in many ways, and we pray to Him many times a day — driving to work, waiting to call on a customer, even washing dishes. Very often we pray and then "see" an answer clearly in our minds, as if someone had "spoken" in a combination of speech and print.

Trying to believe the New Testament was very hard at first, but as God began to work in our lives, we started to see parts of it as literal truth. After six years of growing in the experience of God's love, and learning to trust Him, we find that we now do accept His Word implicitly.

Off to a Bad Start

Our children have shared in all this. There is much more love in the home, and even discipline has come to reflect both love and restraint, firmness and fairness.

Miracles occur, too. One night our nine-year-old was overcome with a virus. She developed a high fever, tossing and turning in bed. Feeling nauseated, she called for a basin, and my wife brought her one and sat beside her for a moment, asking whether they should pray about the illness. "Yes," she said.

My wife placed her hands on the child's head and prayed. In a few moments the fever abated, and the little one went to sleep without another murmur. In the morning her only comment was, "Mommy, I knew God could heal us, but how can He do it so quick?"

We've always seen to it that our children went to Sunday school, but now we know that they did not begin to develop faith and trust in God until we did. They weren't going to be fooled into believing something their parents didn't believe!

Putting faith to work in my business life involved another approach. Since I had my own business, it was comparatively easy, for example, to institute a profit-sharing plan for the employees.

Two years ago one of my salesmen made a serious blunder that would have cost him his job in many companies, but we had faith in the man, and felt that rehabilitation might be effected. I am happy to say our faith was justified, and the man is today a loyal and hardworking asset to the company.

The food business is highly competitive. As a broker, I am sometimes asked to do things for one customer which we are not prepared, or able, to do for others. We try scrupulously to avoid this pitfall, and I believe our customers know this and trust us as a consequence. Letting God be the "senior partner" is not always easy, but I have found that if I do my best with a particular problem, and then take my hands off it and turn it over to God, I cannot quibble with the results.

An added bonus of this way of life is that my stomach no longer gives me trouble, and I can usually leave my business at the office in the evening, go home and relax with my family. Incidentally, for a long time drinking seemed necessary to me because of the social-business customs in which I was involved. Yet situations kept arising and getting out of hand under the influence of liquor — situations that needn't have existed. God seems strangely absent from a cocktail party! It has been quite a few months now since I had a drink. I feel better, and neither business nor social life has "suffered."

Sometimes I wonder why more people don't let God come into their business affairs — and then I remember that just a few years ago I would have laughed at the suggestion of such a possibility. Thank God — and some devoted friends — for helping me to find this way.

To those of you who see something of yourselves in our story, my wife and I would like to emphasize that this transformation has happened not only to us but to many of our friends. It can happen to you, too, because God loves you and wants to be the center of your life. Why not give Him a chance?

Back Together

An easy American divorce was Don's solution to disappointment, and Gwen was faced with the necessity of rebuilding her life and raising the

Off to a Bad Start / 31

> *children alone. Then, through peculiar circumstances, Gwen and Don rediscovered each other.*

Don and I have been married for a little over three years, have never been married to anyone else, and yet have four children, the oldest fourteen years of age. Before you get too shocked, let me explain that we were married, divorced after eleven years, and remarried a year later.

Even before the first wedding our relationship began to break down, because we were basing marriage on the wrong things. I chose Don because he represented financial security and a strong father image, because I was used to him, and deep down, because I wondered if anyone else would want to marry me.

Don, on his part, wanted to marry me to get away from home, and yet he saw in me qualities that would make me a mother to him. The only plus on the ledger was that we were sexually attracted to each other.

With that kind of foundation, things went from fair to bad to worse. I depended far too much on Don; he, obviously, could not find a mother in me. As the children came along, they only made his immaturity more apparent. He couldn't communicate with them on a parent-child basis because he wasn't emotionally grown up himself.

Meanwhile, Don became more and more successful in business. He used this, along with a domineering hand at home, to prove his masculinity. We had the best-behaved children in the neighborhood, but the oldest two were emotional icebergs. Cindy showed this by withdrawing from society. She had no real friends, but buried herself in schoolwork and imitated her father's tyrannical attitude toward her younger brothers and sister. Donnie, the next in line, swung the other way. He was happy only with his peers, avoided adult relationships, and lived for play. And I was too immature myself to cope with the situation.

Without our knowing it, our love for each other and for the children was completely conditional. I loved Don if and when he came home on time for dinner, was nice to the children, polite to my parents, and uncritical of me. He loved me if I kept a spotless house and entertained smoothly.

Don was gradually finding companionship away from the family and was home less and less, until finally he moved out altogether. I was so without stability, direction, and any source of love, that I was almost totally numb.

My younger sister, who belongs to the same church we do, called our pastor and he came to see me. This was the beginning of a friendship and a series of experiences which seemed incredible. My awakening to Christ began — and I thought I had been a Christian for years! Actually, I hadn't even been much of a "churchian." I'd seen to it that the children went to Sunday school, but more often than not I'd skipped the worship services myself.

But now my interest grew and I began to make new friends in the church. I was invited to join a small weekly prayer group where we read Rosalind Rinker's book, *Prayer — Conversing with God*. We experimented with praying aloud in an atmosphere of love and mutual acceptance, believing and expecting definite answers. Month after month we prayed, not that Don would "come to his senses" and return home, but that he might be made more and more miserable until he realized his only help and strength lay in Jesus Christ.

In spite of the anguishing circumstances that surround the process of separation and divorce, God removed from me all feelings of bitterness and hatred. I was maturing as

Off to a Bad Start / 33

a person in my own right, realizing my worth as a child of God — unique and lovable in His sight. So, while I felt no need to "get back" at Don, I no longer needed to be a doormat either.

Slowly and painfully I was learning that I did not need Don in order to be fulfilled. My ultimate dependence was not on him at all, but on God. I learned that I could be a completely free and joyful person in the midst of hellish circumstances. Jesus Christ became a living person to me, and I sensed that God had a definite plan for my life — a fact which needed only my daily affirmation.

Don, meanwhile, was living out his own hell. He finally went to a wonderfully astute psychotherapist who said, "Don, you will get well faster than most because you really want to, and because you are living out your rebellions every day."

When the sources of Don's problems lay before him, and he was beginning to be emptied of many of his frustrations and fears, he was ready to hear the "still, small voice" of God that told him one Saturday evening to call and ask if he could take the children to church the next day. We had not seen Don for many months, so it was a good thing I was sitting down when I answered the phone!

The next morning brought Don's first experience of love in action in the Christian community. After church he was welcomed by many of my friends who knew our story. He wasn't made to feel like the "dog who left that poor girl with four kids to raise," but was loved and accepted just as he was.

For the next seven or eight months Don and I began to rediscover each other. As he related to me what had been going on, I started for the first time to understand what had made him the way he was, and rejoiced with him in his new sense of release. Don saw that I was a different person in many ways, which intrigued him into finding out how this had come about. We went to church together, and he attended our Laymen's Academy with me. In the church we were nurtured in the Christian faith. We experienced together the knowledge that since God loves us where and as we are, we are freed to love each other fully and unconditionally. We now know from personal experience the healing power of God that can change people, and two more hopeless cases it would have been hard to find.

Everyone who attended says that ours was the "wettest" wedding on record. They shared in the deep spirituality of the moment, and there were few dry eyes. Our four children and both sets of parents were seated in the front pew, and heard us exchange our vows, which this time had poignancy and deep meaning for us. This was a marriage not of two but three persons. The bond was complete with Jesus Christ at the head.

The only note of discord occurred when Ray, who was then five, burst into loud howls. It was two or three embarrassing minutes before he could tell me that, of course, he wasn't sorry I had married Daddy again, but that he certainly had expected me to wear a long white bridal gown and veil!

The first year of our new marriage was devoted to being a whole family again and learning to live out the Christian life in our home. This second marriage has love, purpose, and direction because Don and I know who we are and *whose* we are. Our marriage, our children, our church work, Don's business, our money — everything has been committed to Christ, and we are constantly finding more and more to be given over to Him.

Off to a Bad Start / 35

We have discovered our definite and separate roles in marriage. Don's role is to be our guide in spiritual matters, to set policy, to make major decisions, and, above all, to love me as Christ loves His Church. My role is to be the heart of the family, our children's strongest ally and fiercest critic, and a submissive wife, yielding the leadership of the family to my husband.

In these past three years we have just begun to scratch the surface of living what Jesus promises all of us — the abundant life. We still face problems, but we now know where to find the answers. The children have blossomed in an atmosphere where we no longer try to impress our own images on them, but are guided into finding what God has in mind for each one.

Nearly every night while everyone is gathered around the dinner table, we have family devotions. These have produced some marvelous discussions, resulting in a wonderful closeness. All the children participate and have their say on the selected subject, and have a try at memorizing the Bible verse from the devotional book.

Our koinonia group of six couples meets every other Friday evening. We come together for mutual love, support, learning, and service. This completes the circle of what to us are the necessary ingredients of living this abundant life: prayer, the reading of God's Word, fellowship with other Christians, and service to others.

I thank God every day for the miracle of our re-union and for the delightful man to whom I am married. Don has soared way ahead of me, but I enjoy learning from and with him. So, in spite of our parents' embarrassment, we celebrate only the anniversary of our second wedding — it's the one that really counts.

A Christian View of Sex in Marriage

by Bruce Larson*

Recently a friend of mine gave me a copy of "Playboy" magazine with the comment, "You ought to read this. I think the Church has been wrong in its understanding of sex, and Hugh Hefner may have something to say to us Christians."

Well, I read the magazine, and though I cannot agree with Hugh Hefner's philosophy of sex, in which women are objects for man's indulgence, I *can* understand what my friend was reacting against in the Church's traditional attitude. If we must choose between a Victorian view of sex as a necessary evil and the view propounded by Mr. Hefner, we are in an impossible situation.

The position we *can* take is the one we find endorsed over and over again in the Bible. God is the author of sex and it should have as wholesome a function as eating, sleeping, or exercise. It is high time the Church affirmed the *positive* place of sex in God's design for man.

In the "New Morality," modern man reacts against the idea of sex experience only within the confines of marriage. However, the pattern for love is seen in God Himself. God loves man totally and has paid a price because of His love. He is committed to us. Love and commitment are indistinguishable. The Christian position is that love without commitment is dishonest.

But even in marriage the desire to find sexual fulfillment can lead to trauma if either partner feels that he is simply being used to gratify the other without a commitment to

---

*Executive Director, Faith at Work; author of *Dare To Live Now!* and *Setting Men Free*.

Off to a Bad Start / 37

love and to care for his total needs. The legal fact of marriage does not prevent lust, nor does it automatically make sex a creative and satisfying experience. There is nothing in the marriage contract to guarantee that a man and woman will take emotional, financial, social, and psychic responsibility for each other.

However, sex is certainly a barometer in marriage. Is there such a thing as a complete marriage without a satisfying sex life for both partners? I am always suspicious when people tell me they are seeking a "spiritual" marriage. This usually means they hope the marriage will exist on prayer, Bible study, and worship, and sex will be minimal or nonexistent. This is to misunderstand completely what God intends marriage to be.

Even though sex is a barometer, it is not the means to a fulfilling relationship. A mastery of sex technique is *not* the key to a happy marriage, and therefore most books on sexual fulfillment are of little use. The key is rather communication or communion. Sex is not the means to union, but a way of expressing it. It is a language that says, "We are already one mind, one body, one spirit." Couples who fight, bicker, snipe, or sulk all day and then expect to "make up in bed" find that sex does not bridge the gap between two people who are out of communication. A short time spent in confession, asking forgiveness of each other, and prayer can initiate the kind of communion which makes the language of sex natural.

Over the centuries, the Church's stand has been that premarital sex is wrong. This, however, does not vindicate the view that sex is a necessary evil. God's commandments on fornication and adultery are clear. It is because God wants the very best for man that premarital sex has been ruled out. In all my years of counseling, I have never discovered a single married couple who were grateful for their premarital sexual experience. Not one of them felt it was an advantage.

We all know how difficult it is to maintain chastity. In courtship, a healthy sex drive in both partners is normal. To consider marriage with a person who is not struggling with this may be a mistake. What we assume is purity may be psychic frigidity, latent homosexuality, or some other difficult emotional block. When two fairly mature Christians can talk and pray about their sex drives, they're a long way toward solving their problems.

The honeymoon has certainly been misnamed for a great many people, but in this brief period much of the groundwork is laid for the happiness or dissatisfaction which follows. Two people who feel inadequate, insecure, and doubtful about the choice they have made now find that they must "make a go" of the relationship. The finality of marriage creates a pressure which puts panic into the hearts of young people and works against discovering the language of understanding and love.

To avoid this, couples may sometimes feel that premarital sex experience is a helpful thing. But the mystery and joy and wonder of physical union in marriage rests upon the fact of two people learning together as amateurs the physical language of love. The greatest gift God can give two people starting a marriage is a sense of wonder and a sense of humor in approaching this holy and meaningful time. One should not expect to be an expert during the first weeks or even the first months of marriage in communicating the mystery of God's love through sex. For that matter, it is really impossible to approach marriage with "experience." No two people are alike. However much experience

Off to a Bad Start / 39

we have before marriage, we approach a honeymoon as amateurs in the particular relationship.

Many couples have confided that their honeymoon was a pathetic time because each was insecure and felt he did not know enough about the language of love. Later in life, when they experienced God's love in a new way, they were able to take themselves less seriously and to live out that love realistically.

There is no such thing as "an average marriage," in terms of the techniques of love or the frequency of sexual intercourse. Any book indicating that a certain standard is normal is bound to increase the guilt and self-pity in one or both partners. The only rules are the rules of love. Christians have the example of God's own love, and we are free to express love in any way that is meaningful to each other. Under the Lordship of Christ we can throw the rule-book out the window and be led by the law of love.

The frequency of sexual love is often a source of controversy in marriage. Here again books indicate some kind of "normal" schedule for couples of different ages. But what is normal for one partner may seem abnormal for the other, and there is no joy in compromise. It is only as each begins to be sensitive to the other and tries to minister to his needs and demands that union becomes a reality and the physical act becomes an expression of that union.

God wants every couple to have a happy and fulfilling marriage. I am sure Christ is the author of true romance and if we're experiencing Christian marriage, romance and sexual fulfillment should grow richer each year. There is so much sexual disappointment in marriage that many feel, "If only I had married somebody else — possibly that person who is married to my friend or my neighbor — then I would have a satisfying marriage." Strangely enough, love is not something you *do* when you find "the right person." Erich Fromm, the psychiatrist, points out that a painter does not usually waste time searching for "the right object" to paint; he paints whatever is at hand. In the same way, the person who has learned mature love — which is certainly God's love — loves the person to whom he is married without looking around for some mythical "right person."

There is never in any marriage at any given time an equality of desire or appetite. Each of us may change depending on the person to whom we are married and the circumstances of our lives. One friend I know has been married twice. In her first marriage she complained that her husband was too aggressive sexually; now she complains that her second husband is "too cold." Our appetites are subject to circumstance. It is a dream to believe two people can be perfectly attuned in their appetites. In adjusting to the desires of our mate, we learn the true law of love, which is to give rather than to receive.

Extramarital sex is a *result* of a broken marriage, not its *cause*. A satisfied marriage partner seldom strays. It is the duty of each partner to become an instrument in God's hands for the fulfillment of the other. Given enough rejection, we are all potential strayers. If our partner is beginning to stray, we had better examine ourselves to see where we have failed in the law of love.

Finally, it is terribly important for parents to be free to talk about sex with their children. We should help them to understand this great mystery God has placed within us. But if we cannot begin in early years to discuss this with our children, it will become increasingly difficult as they grow older. A friend visiting in our home told us that he had never been able to talk about sex with his parents. One night at the dinner table, he recalled, his sister tried to

Off to a Bad Start

ask where babies came from. She was immediately shushed and the subject was never brought up again in his home. Wistfully, this friend said, "I am convinced that if parents can't talk about sex with their children, they will inevitably lose all communication with them."

This is sadly true. Sex is one of the strongest drives in man, and one of the greatest gifts that God gives to us. If we do not understand and appreciate the mystery and the joy, and if we are not free to discuss it with our children, we have missed a great opportunity and privilege.

II. For Better and for Worse

II. For Better and for Worse

Wishing on a Star

> *In spite of her headlong flight from reality, Marianne could not escape "the same crummy family." Her compulsive eating was only one of the things that drove Mel wild and turned the children into cynics.*

"Can I ask you a question?" whispered our youngest when I tucked him into bed.

"Sure, what is it?"

"Is wishing on a star a prayer?"

"What do you mean?"

He told me, wide-eyed, "One night I saw a bright star, and it reminded me of the star over the manger, and I knew there were angels in that star, so I thought if I wished on the star the angels might hear my wish and take it to God."

As he paused for breath, I asked, "What did you wish?"

"I wished that something might happen to make our family stop fighting, so we'd be happier and have more fun," he said solemnly.

"And when did you make that wish?"

"Just before Christmas."

I looked at my eight-year-old in amazement. Just before Christmas I had read of a workshop in Boston on "renewal in the family." If there was help for our fighting family, I had decided, perhaps I would find it there. And so I had gone, in January, and come back with new faith and hope.

I thought back over all that had happened since. "Yes," I said at last, "wishing on a star was a prayer . . . and I'd like to pray with you now."

All the prayers we had ever prayed before had come from some devotional book, but now I thanked God, quite spontaneously, for giving me a little boy who had the wisdom to wish on a star to find help for his family.

When I finished I was elated. *I've done it,* I said to myself; *my first extemporaneous prayer with one of my family!* But with three boys to keep me in line, I don't have much chance. "That was a nice prayer, Mama," he said curtly. "What book did you get it from?"

Then I thought of my first morning back from Boston. After a seven-hour drive through rain, sleet, and snow, and only three hours of sleep, I groaned from my toes up when our youngest ran in to wake us.

"She'll never make it," my husband announced bitterly. "Better get your own school lunch."

Downstairs, our second son (the "pickle in the middle" who causes all the trouble) could be heard muttering, "Pretty cheap, if you ask me — getting your own lunch."

Yes, pretty cheap, I repeated to myself; *his mother goes off to get religion in Boston. . . .*

"And don't you dare get out of bed until we leave the house," my husband interrupted my musing.

Well, you've never given him any reason to believe you're nice to have around in the morning.

By now I wouldn't have stayed in bed for all the wealth in the world. *You've come back to the same crummy family* — my heart was singing now — *but thank God! Because if they weren't, how could you ever show them you've changed? I have no need to fight back any more. My soul is free* — this from a woman who for years had looked for freedom from the responsibilities of family life . . . looked in books . . . looked in games . . . looked everywhere but in the one place where I could find it — at home.

I bounced out of bed and got out the box of chocolates I'd brought from Boston for the boys. "They're just for you," I explained, "I'm not going to eat even one." (This from a compulsive eater whose weight problem has cluttered the soul of her marriage for sixteen years.) And I didn't, because I hadn't just told myself this time only to retract it later. I told three little boys who counted every piece in the box.

Our perceptive son was baffled. "What's different with you?" he asked. "You don't sound like yourself."

A voice inside warned, *Careful, girl, no religious explanations! Remember, your husband is listening.*

Slowly I formed the answer. "Johnny, I went to Boston . . . to find out what was wrong with our family . . . and I found out the trouble was with me." And to myself I said, *Have I found one place where I can spend one life for Christ? Man, I've come home!*

I put my arms around son number three and told him how much I'd missed him while I was away. I turned to son number two, and for the first time in years his strong, wiry body yielded to my hug and I told him how much I loved him. Son number one, our pimply thirteen-year-old, was missing all this because he was in his room combing his hair for the girls at school.

The January workshop was followed up with a "retreat" in the spring, and to this I went with nostalgic excitement. For one session we were given a list of questions and an hour to ask them of ourselves and to talk them out with God. An hour of silence! Silence can be ominous and oppressive, but this hour was filled with communication with God.

One of the questions hit home: Are you as honest with your own family as you are in your other relationships? My overeating came to mind, and I had to face the fact that I had been honest about it with almost everyone but my husband, Mel. Mel had tried every way he knew to get me to cut down on my eating, but every effort he made only hurt and made me eat even more. I argued with him, "I'm not gaining . . . my clothes still fit."

One Sunday we made ice cream in the old-fashioned hand-turned freezer. I was cleaning up the kitchen later when Mel found me eating all that was left. He looked at me in despair and said just two words, "Oh, no." I was caught in the act.

A voice inside said, *Hold your nose and jump in. The water's fine; it won't hurt a bit.* For the first time I admitted to Mel that I *was* gaining, and I promised him I'd do something about it.

He looked at me in amazement for a moment, then shook his head. "I never thought I'd hear you admit it," he said at last.

But honesty has come easier since. Real freedom results when I can say, "I certainly blew off that time. I'm sorry, and I'll try to be more understanding." Then when I pray I can tell God that I've been trying too hard by myself, instead of being a channel of His love. I make no excuses for myself any more. Because I've experienced God's forgiveness and love it is much easier to ask forgiveness from my family.

Mel told me one day this spring, "I've always felt you wanted me to spend twenty-four hours a day just keeping you happy, and I wasn't going to fall into your trap."

For Better and for Worse / 49

Now we're coming to accept each other as we are, instead of vying to see who can make the other over. The rest and freedom this brings to our marriage is worth every painful, honest recognition of the selfishness and resentment and restlessness that kept me running for fifteen years. I had run from responsibility and from myself to a bowling alley, to bridge games, to a "slimnastic" course (with no diminishing effect on my figure), to drinking coffee by the hour with friends whose lives were as restless as my own — anything and everything to avoid facing myself honestly.

I've learned that as I pray, "God, give me so-and-so," He answers, "Are you willing to give up such-and-such?" As I keep asking and seeking and knocking, He reveals the next resentment or critical attitude that is standing between me and the love He is so willing to give. And despite the fact that I've found out what I'm really like, these have been the most exciting months of my life. I don't feel that I've arrived anywhere, but I've certainly been pointed in the right direction.

Wouldn't it be nice to close this story with, "and they lived happily ever after"? But that isn't the way life is. These past months I've been listening to God and seeing Him work. I've been finding myself — and one by one shedding the masks that I had put on over the years to cover up the insecure little girl I was, until I couldn't even remember the real me.

Mel said recently, "I don't know what happened to you last winter, but I want you to stay this way."

Everything Is Different

After seventeen years "without a quarrel," Anna finally told Jack what she thought was wrong with their marriage. Could his pride recover from the blow — or did they both need to find a new level of understanding?

Jack begins: The draft board was breathing down my neck, so when I flunked out of college, I joined the Marines. I was sent to California, where I met Anna, and in the next nineteen days we had seventeen dates. After I was shipped out to the Pacific, we learned to know and love each other through daily letters. Then, six months later, another fellow wrote me a foul letter about Anna, trying to break us up. Hurt and bewildered, I stopped writing, and my mind was filled with smut.

I needed help. In my sea bag, in an "unused" Gideon New Testament, I found this prayer: "Cleanse the thoughts of our hearts by the inspiration of Thy Holy Spirit. . ." I memorized this prayer and asked God to help me clean up my mind. When Anna's next letter arrived, I was able to accept the logical explanation she offered, and though we were seven thousand miles apart, our relationship was healed. This was my first encounter with a God who could help me in a specific situation.

Anna says: We spent our first year of marriage in the Marine Corps. As Jack attended special training schools, I did nursing in various hospitals across the country. Later Jack returned to finish school at M.I.T., and then he got a job in a steel plant and we moved to Pennsylvania.

Building a home, writing a newspaper column, and caring for three children kept me busy, but after our home was finished I had more time to think about myself, and I became depressed, frustrated, and unhappy. I had a good husband, healthy children, a new house — yet it seemed that I had no purpose in life — no "reason to be."

For Better and for Worse

Pride kept me from telling Jack about my depression and fears, though as a nurse I knew where these symptoms could lead. The big shock came when my doctor prescribed tranquilizers. I thought: *then sleeping pills, then psychoanalysis, then a mental hospital.* I was really afraid.

About this time, Jack's father invited us for a weekend in the mountains, and though Jack wasn't interested, he urged me to go. I packed riding clothes, hiking shoes, a tennis outfit, and the latest best seller. Imagine my shock to find myself at a religious conference! It rained without letup, and there was nothing for me to do but attend the meetings. Surprisingly, I found myself loved and accepted by total strangers, and I couldn't understand it. I listened with awe as people told of experiences of God directing their lives. After the final meeting, I ran to my room, got down on my knees, and prayed. God seemed real to me for the first time. And after returning home, I continued to pray and read the Bible daily, for I had heard many at the conference say how important it was to keep in touch with God. Although I didn't always get much out of this practice, I persisted, for I wanted very much to grow in this experience.

Jack interjects: Anna was on a cloud. For two weeks she went on and on about the conference until I reached the saturation point and told her to shut up. I had not been aware of her unhappiness, though she had been difficult at times. I couldn't understand her praying and Bible study, but obviously something good had happened to her. She became easier to live with, more patient with the children, more loving, and less critical.

Anna resumes: I had to keep quiet, for Jack didn't want to hear what was going on in my life, and the one other person I spoke to about it thought I was losing my mind.

52 / *Marriage is for Living*

The next spring I went to a second conference, and this time I got a penetrating insight into what lay behind my unhappiness and tension: it was guilt — real guilt. I started to read everything I could find on the subject of confession, and after reading *The Healing Light*, by Agnes Sanford, I knew what I must do.

I divided up my life into five periods, and for five successive days took time for a personal inventory of everything I could remember from those periods, writing it all down in an attitude of prayer. The pages filled out, painfully. For the first time I shed tears of real repentance.

I had to clear my conscience of these things which had lain buried for years, so as Easter approached I made an appointment with the chaplain of a nearby college. After a word of explanation I matter-of-factly told him the whole story. "How does this affect your husband?" he asked finally. "Not at all," I said, "he knows nothing about it." The chaplain made no further comment, but took my notebook to destroy it. Then together we prayed through the Lutheran Service of Confession and Absolution.

Afterward there was no special sense of forgiveness, but neither was there any more pressure. I thought: *I've done everything I know how to do.* On Good Friday I went to church, and that night Christ made me aware of His love and forgiveness through an experience of light, warmth, and profound love and joy. From that night on I knew I had been forgiven completely.

Jack backtracks: When the third conference in the mountains came up, I went along with Anna, not quite sure what I was looking for. I was the odd ball in the crowd, for people spoke of Christ as if He were a personal friend. Finally I blurted out to a Canadian medical doctor, "I guess my problem is that I don't believe in Jesus Christ."

For Better and for Worse / 53

"Do you want to?" he asked. "Are you willing to ask Him to come into your life and help you in your unbelief?" Yes, I was willing, though I had many reservations. In the most natural way the doctor prayed with me, as with fear, trembling, and a clenched fist I asked Christ to take control of my life.

Anna and I were together now in a new sense, but at first all I could see ahead was work. *Boy,* I thought, *it's going to be tough to be a Christian!* But soon came another thought: *I don't have to do it myself. The Lord is going to take the burden out of it.* Then I lit up with the joy and release that often accompany an act of commitment. An exciting year followed as Anna and I learned more about Christ and also began to know and work with other Christians.

Anna resumes: Then I reached a kind of stalemate, and wondered why I wasn't growing spiritually. A friend asked how Jack and I were getting along, and I said, "Great, as always. We haven't quarreled in seventeen years." Then he brought me up short with this question: "Doesn't that seem a bit abnormal?"

Suddenly I remembered what the chaplain had said at the time of my confession, and now I poured out some of my story of past sin and guilt. My friend suggested seriously that the time would probably come when I should be as honest with my husband as I had been with the chaplain. Although I feared that I might lose Jack's love and respect, I prayed that God would make me willing to do this if it would result in a deeper faith in Christ and a better relationship with Jack.

Jack interrupts: Now Anna was willing to let me look into her deepest secrets so that I could "know her" in a way I never had. But my pride suffered when she admitted that our marital relations had never been satisfactory to her. For a whole day I lived in hell, wanting to hurt Anna as much as she'd hurt me.

There were some things I could tell her, too! But would I be seeking cleansing — or acting out of spite? I couldn't untangle my motives.

That evening we took a walk together. For the first time I was able to be honest with Anna, and we ended up in each other's arms. Only after this crisis did we discover the wider dimensions possible in a marriage when Christ is allowed to heal both past sins and present failures.

Nowadays when we pray together it is out of a real need, and not simply a conscientious or superficial act. Here's an example of what I mean: I'd been in the Midwest on a Faith at Work team to a parish conference and had driven home with a friend. We had really felt the "breeze" of the Spirit through the long drive, though a blizzard made driving conditions appalling. Finding my car snowbound, I arrived home after hitchhiking the last few miles, still elated and bursting to tell Anna all that had happened.

I came in, kissed the kids, and the first thing little Bradley said was, "Daddy, Mommie drove the Volkswagen through the garage door." Well, I didn't exactly blow my stack, but I did start to cut Anna down to size with snide remarks. After dinner I sat down in the living room, and all the wonderful things I wanted to say were slipping through my fingers. The kids went to bed in stony silence. Finally I said, "Annie, will you pray for me?" We got down on our knees and I just asked to be able to forgive and forget — and that the meanness would leave me. In a quarter of an hour we were back together again in God's own love, and I could share all the experiences of the weekend with her.

Our life has been a process of slow growth, but we have

found in many ways that God is able. For example, at one point we were concerned about our middle child, Peggy, who was going through a difficult phase and going to all kinds of extremes to get attention. I heard some other parents speak of a similar situation with their middle child, and then I was able to put my finger on my own failure with Peggy. What it amounted to was just lack of love. My love was conditional — I didn't love her as she was.

The very next night when I was alone with Peggy I was able to share my discovery with her. I told her I'd been a lousy father and asked her forgiveness. There was consternation on her face as she knelt down with me. When I finished my prayer, Peggy said spontaneously, "Thank You, Lord, for my daddy." This was too much. All I could think was: *Why thank Him for me, when I have been so wrong?* I wept like a child, but it was the beginning of a whole new relationship between Peggy and me.

There are many other stories we could tell to show that faith does work, or rather that Jesus Christ can change the hearts and lives of people today — if they are willing. Everything *is* different!

When the Wine Runs Out

by G. R. Slater[*]

Remember the famous story of the wedding at Cana, when the supply of wine ran out?

In a sense, the wine of marriage always runs out, and there are days of emptiness when the early wine of rapture runs dry, and the promise of a paradise of love fails. But the point which saves the story, and gives us hope, is that

---

[*]Minister, St. Matthew's United Church, Toronto.

Jesus was there to supply what was lacking. The good news is that when Christ comes into marriage and family life, He replenishes what has been used up and exhausted. There is a new quality, a "royal wine," which He makes to flow freely for us.

Alongside this story let us put the portrait of love which St. Paul draws in I Corinthians 13: "Love is patient and kind; love is not jealous or boastful; it is not arrogant or rude. Love does not insist on its own way; it is not irritable or resentful; it does not rejoice at wrong, but rejoices in the right. Love bears all things, believes all things, hopes all things, endures all things. Love never ends." The "royal wine" by which Christ replenishes and fulfills a marriage is none other than this kind of love. When such love enters a marriage, it brings a new spirit, and several things happen:

(1) *It fosters unselfishness.* We have only to look around us to see the pressures which oppose any such altruistic and loving attitude. Exploitation can be found in virtually every sphere of modern life, and in recent years it has laid rude hands upon the highest and greatest gift of all — human personality. Sales people, teachers, executives, television and radio figures are all selling personality as their basic commodity. Erich Fromm has noted that we are a society of consumption: like a great mouth we devour experience and substance. The danger is that we will consume the talents and personalities of people. Now, says Fromm, we have arrived at the point where "sex has become one of the main objects of consumption."

All of this has implications for marriage, for the kind of love which Christ brings is totally opposite to exploitation. It is self-forgetful, self-giving. It cares for the other person as an individual. Luther said that man is the one being

For Better and for Worse / 57

who is "all curled up in himself." The love which Christ inspires draws man out of himself, uncurls him so that he can reach out and genuinely embrace another human being. When this love possesses us, we come to know the other person not just as a means to our own happiness and security, but as a child of God.

(2) *It also fosters realism.* This is love with its eyes wide open. Therefore, it recognizes that no marriage is perfect — which is no news to married people. Realism demands that we recognize the difficulties of marriage; love says we can still have unity through difficulties.

One factor producing trouble is the lack of difference between the roles of husband and wife in our society. Dr. David Mace, who for thirty years has studied marriage around the world, says that in our culture the ideals of democracy have tended to give everyone an equal voice and an equal right to make decisions. It may not be a bad thing that husbands and wives share equally in many areas of responsibility, but it does require a greater love to tolerate the conflicts of opinion and attitude which emerge.

A further difficulty stems from the fact that we are seeking too much from marriage today. Life has become impersonal. Our circle of friends changes often, and there are few long-time friendships. The family has cut itself adrift from formerly close kinship bonds. Now all the closeness and intimacy previously shared in these other ways, among many people, is being focused on *one* person, and the whole load is placed on *one* pair of shoulders — the husband's or the wife's. It is only realistic to recognize the strain that this excessive closeness and extreme demand places upon both husband and wife. One cannot be expected to be mate, brother, father, friend, and psychiatrist all rolled up in one.

When marriage demands this closeness, it reminds us of the dilemma of the porcupine, to use David Mace's illustration. For the sake of warmth and affection porcupines seek to get as close together as possible. But, porcupines being what they are, such closeness does not always give the impression of love. And so they have to draw apart, to leave a space — a "living space" — between them. They find a compromise, a position of equilibrium where they are close enough to be affectionate, but not so close that they hurt each other. Likewise, marriage is a process of getting as close to the other person as possible without injuring or destroying him.

Obviously, there is going to be tension in marriage. When anyone who has been married for many years tells me he has never had an argument with his spouse, I feel like asking, "What's wrong? Don't you care enough to differ? Has communication broken down to that degree? Or is one of you a 'yes-man'?"

Conflict can be creative, and the love which is "patient and kind" is able to embrace tensions creatively in at least two ways:

First, it makes possible an openness and honesty about one's disappointments. Why is it that Christianity is for many a source of guilt rather than strength? Often a person feels that his faith forbids him to be honest or critical with his mate, but you *owe* it to your marriage partner to let him know how you feel. Such openness can be the basis of a new beginning and partnership at a deeper level.

It requires the love that "bears all things" to accept the truth about yourself. Realism demands that you express these feelings within the setting of love and acceptance, for otherwise they will come out elsewhere, and hostility will be vented on the children or on fellow workers.

For Better and for Worse

What is more, the feelings of self-abnegation which prompt a person to suffer in silence rather than risk a confrontation may in fact be destructive. "Love your neighbor as yourself" implies, beyond the obvious, that we are to respect *our own* rights and feelings.

Second, this love that is at liberty to be realistic calls us to recognize that marriage is something that must be worked out. It is not like a coat that is put on, but like a flower that grows. As one elderly lady testified, "Love is what you go through together." It is the recognition, therefore, that you have some needs which are *not* going to be met by the other person, and that there are some things upon which you will *never* totally agree. Realism demands patience and a willingness to adjust. The art of marriage, it has been said, is in maintaining equilibrium through the various changes and adjustments of life together.

(3) *Third, the love which Christ brings into marriage requires a sense of responsibility.* Marriage obligates two people to each other in a final and complete sense. When two young people come to the altar, the minister does not ask them, "Are you in love?" But "Wilt thou love . . . ?" It is not a declaration of how you feel about someone, but a pledge of your fidelity and lifelong loyalty to that person.

It also means responsibility to others. One reason so many marriages founder and fail is that we have not stressed the obligation married people have to society. The students at an American university composed a parody which became the theme song of many couples getting married in the university chapel:

> "We'll build a sweet little nest
> Somewhere out in the West,
> And let the rest of the world go to hell."

It is trite but necessary to say that marriage can never merely be the isolated experience of two people. Like the stone thrown into a pond, its repercussions can be felt on the farthest shore, for good or bad. The same thing holds true of premarital relations.

(4) *Finally, the presence of Christ gives a grace to marriage.* By that I mean a plus, a blessing, and a power beyond the ordinary. It is significant that the marriage of man and woman is the favorite image which the Bible uses for God's relationship to His people. And Jesus spoke of Himself as the bridegroom and the Church as His bride. There is something wonderful about a human relationship which partakes of divine overtones like that.

There *is* something divine in true marriage. It is like a triangle. It takes three to get married — a man, a woman, and God. Francis de Sales put it this way, "If the glue is good, two pieces of wood glued together will cleave so fast to each other that they can be more easily broken in any other place then where they were joined. God glues the husband to the wife with His own blood."

This means that every marriage needs the miracle of God's presence. It needs to invite Him in, so that He can introduce His reconciling grace into the material of two lives. That grace is not a buttress thrown up from the outside to hold up the walls of marriage when they are unable to stand by themselves. It is the "glue" which provides the conditions of personal responsibility, patience, and understanding by which two persons adhere to each other in willing faithfulness.

Driving Without Brakes

Harold drove himself to the limit for community and church. What resources did he have left for

For Better and for Worse

Arlene and the children? A heart attack and an unsolvable problem forced him to find out.

"You can't say no to anybody in this community except your family!"

My wife fled the room in tears of frustration. I had just announced that I'd accepted the chairmanship of a committee to study tax rates for our schools. I had expected a negative reaction from Arlene — already I was spending two or three evenings a week on similar activities — but not *this* much.

After all, I thought, *I'm trying to be an active Christian. Better schools will help my family, so what if it does take me away from them for a while? We're intelligent enough to see "the big picture."* I patched up the quarrel and said I'd try to resign from the committee — but secretly I didn't intend to.

Instead, I soon agreed to something more: running for the school board. It was a logical outcome of the tax study. Why not get into the real policy-making area? Arlene tried hard to go along with this plan, seeing that civic affairs had become my hobby. From the start of our marriage, I had warned her that moderation was not one of my virtues.

The result of this step was more tension — a candidate's worries added to those of a wage-earner, an absentee parent of five children, a spokesman for school tax increases, a Scout adviser, and a Sunday school teacher. I was driving myself to the limit, with no brakes.

The drive mechanism broke down completely three weeks before the election when I had a heart attack. Flat on my back, I "coasted," still hoping to win. I missed by a few votes, but my running mate was elected and the tax measure passed.

In the enforced calm of convalescence, I had time to reflect on the campaign, the frailty of life, and God's purposes. Hurrying and worrying now seemed futile. For example, four days before the attack I had come home from a PTA meeting infuriated and scared because an opposing candidate had had a speaker's spot on the program — giving him, I thought, an advantage. *Getting* the job had become more important than *doing* the job. Now, though the possibility of lifelong invalidism hung over me, I felt a sense of peace. It was a relief to know that no one would ever again expect more from me than I could do.

But even the heart attack wasn't enough to teach me. I decided that if the political arena was too hurly-burly, I would serve God and my fellowmen where it *really* counted — in church. Soon I was a vestryman. At first this promised to fulfill my hopes, but not for long. The practical matters of church finance, mixed with human frailty, produced their own tensions. If anything, "parking-lot politics" was more evident in church than in school affairs! I became thoroughly disillusioned, and eventually resignation from the vestry seemed the only way out.

In the meantime, our children's interests became strongly centered in a new church in the neighborhood, and we finally decided to transfer our membership. Today we have many good friends in both churches, and the harmony God has produced is something I myself could never have engineered.

My lowest point, I suppose, was in the pangs of doubt over leaving one church for another. I believe God permitted me to reach the extremity of realizing that *I couldn't decide* whether it was right. Only then was it possible for me to ask Him to take over and work out the problem harmoniously. From that low point — which proved to be

For Better and for Worse / 63

a real turning-point — God has given back, one by one, each thing that had to be taken away until I could honestly turn to Him for management.

First, physical vigor returned, and I was restored to useful living. Then came the chance to serve on another citizens' group to study our schools' bond needs for new construction. Without rancor, and in the same election that approved the bonds, I was placed in the school board position I had sought before. Our church life, too, became more satisfying, and Arlene and I began to serve as advisers for the high school fellowship.

My work seemed more meaningful — a genuine ministry under God. I have been able to do more accurate work by committing it to Him; to weather occasions of critical questioning of my decisions, and to love my critics; and to witness to my faith in some way almost every day. A noontime prayer fellowship at the plant has become a great spiritual force in my life as I share concerns and joys with fellow employees.

But the greatest boon of all is that our marriage was renewed in a wonderful way. A living symbol of this is Louise, "a happy issue out of all our afflictions," born two years ago.

Then recently a conflict arose between Arlene and me. We were entertaining a visitor, a Christian with unusual insight. We'd all spent the evening in another city, and our visitor was driving us home when I realized I'd inadvertently left my car keys with a friend, and couldn't retrieve the car. After discussing this minor problem, Arlene came up with a plan, which I criticized as naive. Suddenly she turned and said, "You have no faith in my faith!"

This proved to be the key that unlocked much more than the car. At home that night, over a cup of tea, Arlene, our visitor, and I discussed our trouble in communication. She and I each had reasons why the other was at fault. Then we stopped and laughed: my problem was *myself*, and I really had decided her faith was smaller than mine. As a result, I had been setting up unacceptable, impossible standards for her to meet. As our friend said later, I was willing to let God run everybody's life but my wife's.

Beginning right then, we two were able to pray together, confess our faults, and offer our life and conduct to Christ. Our children have been quick to sense the new love and warmth in our marriage relationship, and to respond to it. It has indeed been a new marriage since that moment, thanks to God.

Had anyone told me five years ago what was going to happen and how my life would change, I'd have been very skeptical. Now I have been given back much more than I lost during years of overconcern and conscientiousness.

I'm driving without brakes again, but this time there is *no* concern. God is driving, not I!

Scraping the Bottom

Lucy loved to spend, and Rick had a hard time convincing her that their situation called for restraint. Rick describes the situation:

Money — our lack of it — brought us to Christ.

We moved five years ago from one town to another. In the first community we fit happily into the country club crowd. We lived for golf, parties, and the suburban way of life, swept along by the tide of the town's social elite.

When we moved, we bought a house larger than we could really afford, and then were unable to sell our old

For Better and for Worse / 65

house. Other complications arose simultaneously, our reserve funds were drained, and we were suddenly poor. We couldn't join a country club, so we looked around for things to do.

Before moving we had begun to take our children to Sunday school. We ourselves attended a young couples' class and for the first time were confronted with the Gospel, but we let it roll off our backs. Now we chose a small church for the children which was small and friendly. When people tried to get *us* involved, we replied, "We'll join your bowling league, but no discussion groups, please!" We weren't opposed to people being Christians. In fact, we rather thought we'd like to be Christians sometime, but not just now.

Up the street lived Andy and Lois, who held small group meetings in their home. Lois kept inviting us each week, but we had all kinds of excuses not to go. Finally she said to Lucy, "If I'm boring you I won't ask again."

Lucy was too "chicken" to admit the truth, but replied instead, "Oh, no, I was really planning to come tonight." As a result, we both went and kept going. It was through this group of people that we committed our lives to Christ. It was the first time Christianity had appeared alive to us.

Now, five years later, we still haven't joined the country club. Maybe someday we will, but right now we feel it would be a waste of money. We wouldn't get that much golf in. The Lord has moved into our lives, and we have found out what is important. What would have gone for many of the unnecessary luxuries now goes to the church and related activities.

We have learned in the group to communicate better between ourselves. Communication, not money, has really been our problem all along. When we got married we discovered we had different attitudes toward money, but weren't able to talk about them. My father had almost lost his business in the depression, and money was talked about a lot in the family, so to me planning carefully and budgeting were important. But to Lucy, whose father had drawn a steady paycheck all through the years and consequently was not much affected by the depression, the money had always been "there" and could be depended on. She felt there was no need to budget, and my questions about her spending made her feel persecuted.

There were frequent emotional outbursts at the end of the month — bill-paying time — when I would accuse Lucy of throwing money away. A crisis came the first Christmas in our new house. Here's how it sounded:

Lucy: How much can we spend for Christmas?

Rick: If we stretch it, we can spare fifty dollars.

Lucy: Fifty dollars! Why, I used to spend that much by myself when I was in high school!

Rick: Well, here's the checkbook. See for yourself.

So we had Christmas for fifty dollars — with three children — and discovered it was possible. We didn't send many cards that year, but we did have a tree. Some neighbors who were going away for the holiday asked if we'd like to have their tree — and they didn't even know our financial situation!

In the group, as I said, we've learned to communicate. Among friends who have similar problems it is somehow easier for us to talk to each other more objectively and without offending. Often when the door is shut between us, we find door-openers at a group meeting. Now the two of us talk through what we're going to do with our money: what we're going to spend it on and how much we're going to give away. We feel an obligation to share what we have

For Better and for Worse

with other people. We still have no formal budget, and there are still occasional crises, but there's clear understanding between us as to how our money is to be used. All of it is spoken for, so writing the checks each month becomes almost automatic.

We know now how unimportant money is. The most valuable things in life can't be bought. We discovered that last spring when we took two children into our home from a family that had broken up. Those kids were starved for love, though they had better clothes and more toys than our own kids. At first I was embarrassed when their father visited because of the fancy toys he kept bringing. Then I discovered that it was the only way he had of relating to his children. I tried to tell him that what his kids needed was assurance of love, and that *things* couldn't provide this.

One thing I feel very strongly against is getting overextended by buying on credit. But I'm glad now that we went overboard on the house. If we'd moved into a cheaper one, we may have felt we could afford to join the country club — and for all we know we'd still be out there playing golf, but not really living.

III. When the Jitters Take Over

III. When the Jitters Take Over

The End of the Rope

With one marriage failure already chalked up against him, rough-and-tumble Joe couldn't take it when Thea started to pack her bags. There was only one place to turn for help.

I was about sixteen when I went on my own and began to devote myself to a life of conscious self-interest. After finishing high school, I ran away and got married. My main interests were making money, drinking as much as possible, and not letting anything or anyone — including my wife and three children — interfere with my pleasure. After ten years my wife gave up and filed suit for divorce.

Then, on a shoestring, I went into the trucking business. In spite of my heavy drinking, through hard work and tenacity the business was built up. Along with this legitimate enterprise I had a lot of shady deals on the side — like taking bets on horse-racing. Anything to make a dollar. I guess I was the picture of a hard-driving, hard-living, self-made man.

My second wife, Thea, was an asset to the business as well as a wonderful person. She was not as materialistic as I was, but together we poured ourselves out for this dream of "success." At the same time we began to raise a family of four boys.

Our home life was rocky. Somehow Thea managed to stay close to God, and from time to time she would beg me to pray about my drinking and the rough stuff I'd pull when I was drunk. Instead of praying I'd promise to "do better," but my resolutions consisted of compromises. I would drink less for a while, then forget my promise, go on a tear, come home and abuse my wife and kids, and the next day not even remember it.

We settled in a beautiful new home, joined the country club, and I discovered that boozing it up with this set was pretty much the same as my "lost weekends" along the Bowery of New York City. No new house, no country club, and no amount of money was sufficient to make us happy or to keep us together.

At last Thea reached the end of her rope, and informed me that she had "had it" and was going to move out. This shook me up. While my wife was packing her things I went off by myself, wondering what in the world I could do. I wasn't a church-going man, except once or twice a year, and didn't pray. But I remembered my childhood training at home, when we had been active in a church and had regularly held family devotions, and the thought came: *If I ask God to come into my life and take over, He will.*

Don't ask me why, but I believed this. I had thought about it each time I made a resolution to "do better," but had never taken the step because I knew what it would cost. I knew it would mean definitely giving up the right to run my own life, and asking Christ to run it for me — and I was afraid of the consequences.

But now, backed into a corner, I could see no other way. I got down on my knees and prayed. Then I told Thea what I had done, and she had the courage and the faith to believe me. She stayed, though doctors and psychiatrists she had consulted strongly urged her to leave me before it was too late. More than once I had beat her up, and one

When the Jitters Take Over / 73

time I had actually locked her out of the house in the middle of the night.

Shortly after this crisis in which Thea agreed to give me one last chance, I became involved in church life, and came to know the minister. It didn't take long for "the Rev." to persuade me to start a men's Bible class in my home on Wednesday evenings. We also began to have family devotions every night, in which even the eight-year-old could take part.

After my initial commitment to Christ, I soon found out that the life He gives has to be given away. Christianity is not just a matter of "being good." It's a dynamic thing that changes all our attitudes — toward family, work, the community, the world. For example, in many businesses today there are angles to figure, ways to cut corners and cheat — nothing too drastic, understand — to pick up a few extra bucks. The trucking business is no exception, and after twenty-one years in trucking I know the angles.

I started to hear about a different way: about businesses where prayer and faith played a part. Finally it got through to me that we could try this, too. One day I called the men in — there are at least twelve at all times, and in busy seasons as many as eighteen — and said I had the conviction that we should start our day with prayer together. We started in a simple way, just asking God to guide us through the day, and praying that we would be able to love each other and not be critical. Later we added other kinds of prayer; intercession for those who were ill or in trouble, for example.

Gradually a change took place. There was less bickering, less buck-passing, more acceptance of responsibility, better personal relations.

Not that problems stopped coming up. What do you do,

for instance, when you find out that one of your employees has padded a repair bill and pocketed the difference between the actual cost and the figure he quotes? What do you do a few months later when the same man goes haywire on a cross-country trip and blows nearly four thousand dollars of company money?

The easy thing is to fire the man, collect what you can from the bonding company, and forget it. But nowadays I find it harder and harder to take the easy way out. I ask myself, "Who am I to condemn him when I know I'm not condemned for all the stupid things I've done myself?"

So you try to get close to the man, find out what's missing in his life that prompts him to do these things, keep him on the job, and give him a chance to make restitution and go on from there. And you give him a picture of your own life, and say honestly and naturally that when Christ takes control of a man everything changes. Then you try to get him involved in a men's Bible class, urge him to go back to his church, and to get his family life straightened out.

I hope this doesn't make me sound like some kind of authority on personal rehabilitation. I'm not an authority on anything. All I know is what's happened to me.

And I've made plenty of mistakes in trying to "witness" — with my own son, for instance. Rod is the oldest, and he has a family of his own. I kept trying to coerce him into going to church and praying. A problem came up at the office one day and Rod cracked, "Do it Dad's way; don't work, just pray."

Finally I saw that I was hounding him, and took the pressure off. Leaving him in the Lord's hands was the right way, after all. A few months ago Rod heard a speaker who made a powerful impact on him. "I closed my eyes, Dad, and saw Christ standing right there," he told me. Shortly afterward, he went to church one evening and made a public profession of faith.

I guess it's easy to see why I'm enthusiastic. The Lord is good, and I can't keep quiet about what He's done for me. I'm very grateful for my wife's faith all through the years. She stuck with me when there was no human reason to do so.

Of course I can't help regretting all the time I wasted, and all the people I hurt. I hope there will be opportunities to make up for these things. But I'm thankful to worship the Lord in whom there is no condemnation. He never throws a man to the dogs — and we can't, either.

My Screaming, Hateful Self

How do you go about admitting that you hate your children? The tension mounted and Alice told herself, "Someday I'm going to snap."

I was "a bundle of nerves." Having four pre-school children around all the time was more than I could take. We had wanted all the children, and had wanted them close together in age, but the strain was more than I had bargained for.

Some mothers seem to manage such a situation easily, but for me it was impossible. I was a perfectionist — well-organized, independent, self-sufficient. Children, however, are not pieces of furniture to be rearranged at will. The clashing of our self-centered personalities created chaos in our home. I was less and less in control, and getting to the point where resentment turned to hatred.

My husband thought I should see a psychiatrist, but I resisted. As for my devotional life, it was sad. I had given up routine prayers long ago, but for five years I'd attended a Sunday morning Bible class, looking for "a reason for the faith that was in me." I learned a lot of facts, but God never became real to me. I read the Bible critically, picking it apart until it seemed dead.

So I tried to get back into the habit of prayer, getting up early for a pre-breakfast walk. At least I was awake! My husband and I went to a discussion group, and there we met Sara and Henry, a young couple who were friends of Adeline, the Director of Religious Education at our church. I looked at Sara with skeptical curiosity when several times she said things like "all the things the Lord has done for me." I wondered what those things were.

During the summer the group didn't meet, but I taught Vacation Church School. I was annoyed with the material we had to teach. In fact, I wrote out a long criticism of it and sent it to Adeline, saying, "It is far too idealistic. A Christian doesn't have any more patience, self-control, or love than the next fellow."

Adeline came to see me as soon as she read my comments. She gave me a sermon on grace by S. M. Shoemaker, and suggested that we might attend a Faith at Work conference in September. She also advised me to talk to Sara, who had faced problems similar to mine.

I went to the conference, a bit skeptically. Yes, I wanted what those people had, but I had "committed my life to Christ" before and "nothing had happened." Still, it couldn't hurt to try again.

I came home feeling inspired for a few days, but soon became my screaming, hateful self again. One morning was particularly bad, and I was so upset that I thought, *Someday I'm going to snap, and I really don't think it's far away.* I was crying hysterically, calling out to God that if He was

When the Jitters Take Over / 77

going to help me it had better be soon, for I was at rock bottom and couldn't help myself.

After I'd calmed down I called Sara, and she came right over. That morning I sat down and made a list of all the things that were wrong in my life. I was surprised at how many there were. Sara talked with me as we went over the list, and together in prayer we turned them all over to God, asking Him to come in and take control.

I'd never confessed my sins to another person, and on thinking it over I realized I'd never had a *conviction* of sin before. I could remember saying that I couldn't feel very sorry about being a sinner because the very fact that I was a human being kept me from being anything else. It was this attitude which had invalidated my previous attempts to let God control my life.

I wish I could say that from that moment all was rosy, but the fact is I moved very slowly. I felt better but seemed to be in a kind of trance, wanting something to happen but very skeptical that it would.

We started going to a fellowship group, and they said to me, "It *has* happened; don't doubt it, but thank God for it." Soon I became more hopeful.

Then one day I had a real test, with my four children and four others in the house from the middle of the afternoon until nine in the evening — usually the worst time of day for me. I came through calm, cool, and collected.

The next morning another friend called to ask me to mind the baby for her, and I prayed quietly, "Okay, God. You don't have to convince me any more that You're with me." I found myself filled with joy for no particular reason, handling difficult situations in the right way, whereas before I would have blown up.

Hymns started to "speak to me." Sermons were alive.

What I read in the Bible hit me between the eyes. It was like going from blindness to light. I wanted to tell everyone, but found this difficult, especially with close friends. Few people knew of the inner turmoil that had brought this about. After all, you don't broadcast the fact that you hate your children. Rather, you put a good face on it and pretend everything is all right.

Some time later I "hit a snag," and then realized there were some things God wanted me to change. I wasn't anxious to do so. He wouldn't settle for half a life; He wanted all. Because I'd been so accustomed to a self-centered existence, God had to wrestle with me, and still does sometimes.

But He is changing my ideas, my attitude toward money, and the way I spend my time. He has gotten through to me that the important things in this life are *people*, not things. Before, I didn't care, didn't need people, and didn't want to get "involved."

I'll continue to stumble, but now I have a faith that is real and vital, and I know I'll get up again. I believe in the power of prayer because I have seen it work time and again. I don't know what God has planned for me, but I shall try to "keep the lines open" and to obey, with His help and the help of other committed Christians.

Why Opposites Attract

by Lionel A. Whiston[*]

There is more truth than poetry in the old saw, "Opposites attract," for a man will often be attracted to a woman who demonstrates personality traits he himself lacks. Uncon-

---

[*]Congregational Minister, Wrentham, Massachusetts.

When the Jitters Take Over

sciously we seek fulfillment in the one who personifies what we do not possess, and therefore deeply long for. Thus the extrovert is drawn to the calm and quiet type, the rationalizer falls in love with the sentimentalist, and the practical person marries the dreamer. By and large, persons of *like ideals* are attracted to each other, and most often those of similar cultural backgrounds, but in the realm of temperament opposites seek each other out.

When opposites marry, there is a potential both for growth and deterioration of the individual personalities. Sadly, it is sometimes easier to bring out the worst in a partner than the best.

Picture a self-contained, reflective man, given to choosing his words carefully, who marries a girl of ready wit and tongue, quick on the trigger and vibrant to her fingertips. One autumn they are visiting friends and the hostess says, "Bill, what did you folks do this summer?" Bill pauses to consider which of several things might be most interesting to tell, but his wife Sue has already launched into a graphic description of a school of whales they had seen off the coast of Maine.

As this type of incident is repeated many times in many forms, dire things happen. Bill becomes more and more taciturn. He begins to doubt himself, feels increasingly inferior, becomes afraid to take part in conversation, and finally wonders whether his ideas are important after all. More serious than this is his growing bitterness. Reacting to Sue's aggressiveness, he says in his heart, "Okay, Old Girl; go ahead and answer for me. See if I care!" But he *does* care, and his resentment grows.

Sue is oblivious of all this. All her life she has been something of a show-off, though not offensively so. More and more she "takes over" for her husband, and if she thinks about it at all, she simply regards her action as saving him energy "after a hard day's work." Unconsciously she takes the center of the stage and dominates the situation, completely unaware of the damage that is being done both to Bill's personality and to her own.

Then one day Bill finds the courage to open his heart to Sue — the most difficult thing he has ever done. Why is it so hard to be transparent with his own wife? There is a strange ambivalence: he both *wants* and *dreads to be known*. Deep calls to deep, and he longs to be one with Sue in heart and mind; yet he is afraid that if Sue really knows him, she will not love him any more. He fears that his strong masculine image will be shattered, and Sue's love and respect will fade.

So much conspires to make the telling difficult! But finally he takes the plunge and expresses his fears and inadequacies, his loneliness and sense of inferiority, his lust and pride, his desire to be praised and flattered, and his unfulfilled need to be noticed — to take center stage.

The unexpected happens. Sue listens in amazement, and when Bill is all through she says, "How can I change so that it will be easier for you to be open with me, like this, from now on?"

Deep fellowship begins. It is the start of a new and wonderful relationship. They begin to bring out the best in each other instead of the worst. Sue, surprised at how often she has asserted herself, holds back and becomes more aware of the needs of others. Slowly she learns the art of listening in love.

For Bill, too, change is hard, for he has become secretive, self-contained, and cowardly. But now, encouraged by Sue, he speaks out and is willing to have his ideas challenged.

° ° °

When the Jitters Take Over / 81

In marriage it often happens that one partner is a good listener while the other does most of the talking. Listening and conversation are both arts, and both need cultivating. The story of Bill and Sue — a true story — illustrates the value of forthright conversation and deep listening, and the importance of willingness on the part of married couples to relate their own authentic inner experiences. Couples who are growing together need often to talk through their ideas and ideals with openness and transparency. When verbalized, things are seen in a different, often a truer, light. An honest confrontation rubs off rough edges and reveals hidden irrationalities.

To speak in love, to discuss in good temper, to explore ideas without competitive or argumentative spirit, indicate maturity in marriage. Wisdom usually dictates that the time to talk is not during the period of crisis or pressure, but when tempers are cool, hearts are open, and insights honestly and willingly expressed.

The art of listening is even more crucial. Have you ever sat on the edge of a chair waiting for your partner to pause for breath in order to get in a word of advice, an argument, a point of view? A person may easily want to win his argument regardless of what it does to his mate. Such an attitude makes it impossible to hear what the other person is really saying.

One needs to listen not only to the spoken word, but to the unexpressed thoughts and desires of his marriage partner. All of us are guilty at times of hiding our real thoughts or purposes.

Imagine a man coming home from work, tired and discouraged, saying, "Everything went wrong today." How easy it is for his wife to hear only these words, and for her curiosity to prompt the response, "What happened?"

The wise wife tries also to "hear" the unspoken thoughts: *I'm not as capable as I should be*, or *I'm not as good a provider as my family needs*, or *I'll lay for that fellow tomorrow and really get him!* Then, if she knows her husband well and recognizes unspoken overtones, she will find some way to give him supportive love. Perhaps she should not ask, "What happened?" but simply put her arms around her husband and let him know he is Number One to her.

° ° °

Because we differ so widely in ideas and behavior patterns, our tendency is to try to change and make over our mates. How tragically common is this type of harangue: "Why do you have to come home so grouchy? Jim Smith doesn't . . . his wife said so! And what's more, he always looks neat and well groomed, and he doesn't make any more money than you do!"

Or, from the husband: "Where on earth do you spend your afternoons? Don't you ever clean house? And why is it every day I'm greeted with, 'You'll have to punish Johnny, he's been. . . .'"

Slowly but surely John and Mary build up fantasy images of the kind of partner each would like to have. Each dwells on what joy it would be "If John were only. . . ." — "If Mary would just. . . ." How comforting it is to set up a dream image! We can mould it at will, make it conform to our slightest whim. It satisfies our egos to play God and re-create our partners. It involves no costly change, for it is flight from reality. Instead of coming to grips with life, we escape into wishful thinking and vague hopes.

In this kind of situation, one falls more and more in love with the fantasy image, and by the same token falls more and more out of love with his real life partner, and con-

When the Jitters Take Over / 83

sequently with real life itself. When love is inhibited, blocked, or deflected, it turns sour, and its energy is transformed into negative emotion, even hostility. An old song expresses this common experience: "You always hurt the one you love."

If we could love purely, with God's kind of love, we would both *love people as they are* and *set them free*.

For years a wife has been urging, at times even nagging, her husband to get a raise. Finally it comes, and her happiness is unbounded. "Darling, this is wonderful. I'm so proud of you! Let's go out tonight and celebrate."

"I guess not, Honey," is his reply, "I've got a date with some of the boys from the office." The wife is crushed, not realizing that her nagging has taken the joy out of her husband's achievement long before it came. As for him, he may not even be fully aware of the reasons why he would rather share his satisfaction with the boys from the office than with his wife. The truth, of course, is that he needs to be loved *for himself*, and not for the money he brings home.

When we seek to make over our partners, we set up resistance in them. The design may be open pressure and scolding, temper or tears, or even subtle acts like leaving a book open to some significant passage or asking loaded questions. Sometimes, through persistence, we succeed in changing another person's behavior, but this seldom effects an inner change of spirit.

The crux of the matter lies in the answer to the question: In what do we put our trust? Is it in our cleverness and ability to bring about a change in people through our wits, planning, suasion, and subtle force? Or are we ready to trust God's kind of love and this alone? One day a friend of mine admitted, "I said to God, 'God, you love my husband and I'll change him.' But God said to me, 'Louise, *you* love your husband and *I'll* change him.'"

God is both love and reality. He loves us as we are, yet His love reaches to the real person within each of us. Because He is God, He loves His children as they are, asking that they respond to this love, but in the meantime setting them free to be themselves, to accept or to reject.

There is great power in the love of God because it is not given on condition of our responding to it. It is given freely, regardless of what we do. "The rain falls on the just and the unjust."

Man's love is different, for he loves where he gets the greatest return. People who are grateful get more of his love than people who are ungrateful. Man's love is often a reaction to someone else's behavior, and its flow is conditioned by the other's reception and response. On the other hand, God does not react to us: *He acts,* constantly and continuously, with unconditional love.

In marriage, to love with God's kind of love is to see one's spouse through God's eyes, as it were, as deeply lovable. It is to love him regardless of his reactions. It is to set him free to be himself, even to resist and rebel against our love if he so chooses.

There is power in this kind of love, but it must be shown wisely — never as smothering, oppressive, or demanding. St. Paul prayed that our love be a wise love, growing in knowledge and wisdom (Philippians 1:9). Love needs a deft touch. It needs to know the time for humor and small talk, as well as the time for intent listening or speaking from the depths of the heart.

God's love has no ulterior motive. Ours is often calculated to bring results. When the desired results are not forthcoming, how pained or resentful we can become! "I

When the Jitters Take Over

spent hours preparing that dinner, and you pick at it!" "If you knew how I scrimped and saved to buy you that coat, maybe you'd wear it once in a while!" But God's love has no angle; it is sheer love, let loose among men for them to embrace or crucify.

Our hope should not be to affect the outward behavior and ethical conduct of our marriage partners, but rather to touch the inner self. Paul said that we are to let our minds be remade and our whole nature transformed. After that, outward behavior will follow whereby we will do the good and acceptable and perfect will of God (Romans 12:2). It is important to remember that the changing of the inner nature is God's job, not ours. Like a little child with his first garden, we want to "pull up the beans to see how they're doing, and hustle them along."

What can we do to make possible an inner change? We must set a partner free so that our pressures will not inspire resistance in him, nor our desires entice or drive him to a different course of action "just to please us." How often we hear such a sentence as: "I should think you'd do this just because I asked you to, if for no other reason."

It is sometimes difficult to like and love a person *as he is* precisely because it is difficult to separate a person from his behavior. Yet a person can be lovable and likeable even though his conduct is irritating or repulsive. It takes grace, but it can be done. God separates the sin and the sinner, for surely this is the message that Jesus brought us about the love of God.

In honoring the personhood of our partners, it is essential that we trust them to hear, and ultimately to respond to, God's word for them. This involves standing by them even when they refuse to hear, or hear "wrongly." It means being patient though they may blunder and fall again and again. It means being willing to be free of judgment and self-righteousness as our partners struggle and grow and experience. The key is daily consciousness of our own need to grow in the way of God's love, and of our own fallibility.

Why Me, Lord?

> *It didn't seem fair. All the other young couples in the neighborhood had children — sometimes more than they really wanted. But not Candace and Murray. For them, only disappointment.*

About four years ago, I lost what would have been our first baby. My husband and I became reconciled to our loss, as most young people do in such circumstances, especially as my doctor assured us he knew of no reason why our hopes for a family might not be realized without any special delay.

I'm afraid my attitude of acceptance depended quite a bit, however, upon a condition — the granting to us of another baby *immediately*. Then two years passed. I consulted the doctor at regular intervals, only to be told finally of a new, negative factor affecting my chance of becoming a mother: I wanted a child so intensely that within myself a condition was created which worked against this goal.

I became so angry with the doctor (as if it were his fault) that I vowed not to consult him again. So another year passed during which my desire for motherhood remained as strong as ever, while my impatience and rebellion increased. I was becoming deeply frustrated and neurotic, and on several occasions burst into tears of resentment when told that a friend was expecting a baby.

During that period, my husband Murray was most un-

When the Jitters Take Over / 87

derstanding and forgiving. If he had not been, I'm sure that my depression and resentment, which precipitated many crises in our home life, would have wrecked our marriage. My uncontrolled feelings sometimes turned against him, though for the most part it was a deep-seated sense of personal inadequacy which troubled me.

Finally I began to see what harm my attitudes were doing, but I also realized that I knew very little about how to correct the situation. I had tried praying that God would send us a baby. Since He had not done so, my attitude toward prayer became negative. I had also kept myself busy, with the idea that less time to think might help. I had even enrolled as a full-time college student!

The most that happened through these self-cure measures was that I pushed the frustration back into my mind, telling myself I really didn't care about a baby after all. Of course I knew this was not honest, but at least it made things better on the surface.

Then came the turning-point. The minister at our church started holding weekly fellowship meetings with several young couples who wanted guidance in faith and communion with God. We were invited to join, and we went to our first meeting just over a year ago. I intended only to listen, but even at that first meeting, I was moved to tell my story and to ask for help.

As a group, we discussed how to pray, and the steps which were necessary to make prayer effective. Before I left I had a different feeling about prayer and about myself. I knew I had been praying with a closed and bitter heart, and because I had not been honest with myself I had shut out God.

I stayed with this group and learned how to pray. For the first time I asked God to take over the situation which troubled me so much. I still wanted a baby, but I prayed that God would enter my heart and make me willing to accept whatever was His will.

Within a few months my frustration and resentment disappeared, and I became free of urgency. The desire itself had not disappeared, but God had given me patience, and I was willing to allow Him to work His will in me.

No doubt Murray was even more delighted than I at the change in my attitude. At last I was at peace; I knew my problem was in better hands than mine, and that I could be content to let God work it out and not quarrel with His decision.

This was a miracle in itself, but it was just the beginning. As I write, we are joyously expecting a baby in July.

My husband and I have not been so happy and content for years. I know that I have only made a beginning, but I can testify that faith does work.

A Day (Un)Like Any Other

How much can happen in a single day to a man and woman who see that they have built their house on sand, and that the foundations are beginning to crack?

This is the story of a single day — a day begun as any other, but marking at its close the definite end of one kind of life and the start of another.

Two lives were involved in this Tuesday — the lives of two spoiled children — nice, comfortable lives following lines of least resistance; responsibilities almost unknowingly shirked; emotional immaturity; selfishness — and here is the punchline — *sin*.

When the Jitters Take Over / 89

Until this Tuesday, the girl in this story had never thought of sin except in its most general sense. Of course she knew she had sinned, but since that Tuesday she has been able to say, "I have sinned," and then to leave off the "but."

She and her husband started their marriage with the Grade A handicap of two divorces — one apiece. They had entered marriage soberly and with high hopes, but with sadness in their hearts, too. They both had children from whom they were separated. It was something they didn't talk about much, but it gnawed — my, how it gnawed!

They knew it would take a very deep and enduring love to get them over this hump of separation from those to whom, and for whom, they were responsible, but they thought they could manage it — just the two of them. They started out; he had a big job and she got a small one. It kept her busy until the evening rolled around and they could be together.

Things went along with a nice glossy surface until the big job began to fall to pieces. The jitters held full sway and doctor bills began to come in like Christmas cards. She was a good nurse, competent and self-sufficient, but given to waking up in the night, walking the floor and wondering how soon one lost consciousness in a jump from the fifteenth-story window. Outwardly, all love and devotion; inwardly, a bowl of unset jello.

This phase passed. They went to church regularly. They prayed for things and people. They set their eyes on a stone figure of Christ and that was all they saw.

Then along came another job, a real one this time. "It'll mean being separated, but it's a big opportunity," said he. "You hop to it — it's your big chance," said the little woman, being of unsound mind but noble character. So he went and she stayed — lonelier than she had ever thought it possible to be lonely, miserable and afraid, and sorry for herself to the extent that she wore black, figuratively and literally. And the new job? Pressure — temper — all-night sessions — a bunch of dimwits to work with — "get this assignment out by the 17th" — "no system" — and so it went.

A part of this job, however, was back in the home town, so the home fires burned a little more brightly. Something was going, though — something was gone — or had it ever been there in the first place? It wasn't that she was better than he; she just had more time to think and worry.

Then an even larger opportunity came: the promise of a partnership. Flattering, too, and from the top three bosses. Of course it involved travel for eight months out of the year, but anytime she got too lonely the company stood ready to treat her to a trip to whatever far-flung field of competition held her husband at the time.

She began to pray in earnest: "Don't take him away. Please keep him here with me. I can't get along alone — I've given up every single thing for him — I have no one else." That prayer went unanswered to the ceiling at least fifty times a day, because he made his decision to go. "The next ten years must be given to making money — money to help parents — money to send to the children" — money to make him forget. That was it. It came to her in the early hours that Tuesday. *He was running away.* He was in real, personal conflict about having to go, but go he must. Money was all that was needed.

Then she began to see things. She looked at him closely and saw that he was in real mental and spiritual need — just as she was. She had clung to him so closely, so selfishly, that she had been too near to see him at all. She began to see the indecision in his eyes and the "gone" look to his shoulders.

When the Jitters Take Over / 91

Then and there her prayer came out in a different version: "God help *him*. Take me out of this. Think of him now and his needs. He needs You — and I know You need him, too. Use him. Make Your will known to him and whatever it is, I'll stand by it. And bring us both to a living consciousness of You."

This was Tuesday, and this was the girl who had laughed a little at God's ability to guide in personal matters. She didn't exactly ask for guidance, but she got it. As her husband walked down the street, she went into the bathroom and brushed her teeth, then dashed into the bedroom and got down on her knees — an unprecedented event in the annals of her life. Then she went straight to the phone and made a call. This call was to someone through whom she knew God could work, just as He was working through her at that moment. It all seemed a kind of solemn magic: no fanfare, no revelation in a fiery cloud, no lights, no music — but something inside that had to be obeyed and something or Someone giving orders.

She sat there after she had hung up the phone and chewed on her favorite fingernail. A little of the old confusion crept into her thinking. "If God does tell him to resign this position and get out from under, it's going to take tremendous courage to face those three tycoons. And if he does resign, there certainly isn't anything else in the offing. There was that other job — the one I really wanted him to take. He could have been of real service there. Well, they probably had someone else by now. . . ."

The "service" angle of the work he had turned down hadn't appealed to her until Tuesday. She'd wanted it because it meant he would stay at home. But now she saw what a real chance it would have been. Why, it was work for children — boys — not their own, certainly, but other boys who needed help in maladjusted surroundings — unhappy homes. The full force of it struck her now and she felt it more deeply each moment. Well, whatever happened just must be.

Not until noon did she know anything more, but someway she didn't *need* to know. She went back to work, and she came back to hear over the telephone a well-loved voice — a quiet voice — say that he had resigned. He had talked the thing out with a friend — *and with God!* — and had gone straight to the lions and bearded them!

"Were they angry . . ."

"Not at all."

"What did you say?"

"I told them I had been down on my knees about the whole matter."

"What did they say to that?"

"That it wasn't often that a man was willing to face his God about a job."

"And now what?" — and she almost laughed — "You are completely and wonderfully out of a job at all."

"A funny thing happened," he answered. "When I told the chief all this, he asked me what my plans were and I admitted I had none; that I had closed the door on the only other opportunity. Then he said, 'Nonsense. If you want that other job, I can help you get it.'"

Here was one for the book: the comic-strip boss would have blown up and stormed at all this inconvenience. He'd have said, "Get out, you young numbskull. You don't know your own mind. Get out, and don't come back." And the husband's boss had been known to do just that. Could it be that God had reached down a little in this instance, too? It was all very strange — and yet most natural.

And that's about all of this story — so far. The new job

has begun, and it's the one for the children. Of course it is only a beginning for these two people, and not a wholly easy one, either. It isn't easy for them to recapture, day by day, the magic of that Tuesday. Neither of them had been a believer in sudden conversion, at least not for themselves, and so this very real experience has meant a shifting of their values and foundations.

Each of these persons has faced his sins — bitter pills they have been, too. None is forgotten, but they feel the sins have been forgiven by God. And more and more often Christ is entering into that picture; in small ways, perhaps, at first, so that later there may be bigger occasions in which He can touch their lives and the lives of those around them. They know now that it takes time and thought and courage and discipline to be a real person — a person committed to Christ and to the kind of living He demands — not just on Tuesday, but every day, hour, and minute of their lives.

Marriage Is Four Strands

by Walden Howard[*]

Marriage is like a rope — not a rope with which to hang yourself, despite cynical jokes such as, "Marriage isn't a word it's a sentence" — but a rope uniting two lives in one.

A rope, the dictionary says, is "a strong, thick cord made by twisting smaller cords together." The rope of marriage is made up of four strands that must be woven with loving care by the two who enter into its promises.

Marriage doesn't *happen,* any more than the strands of a rope automatically come together in their place. A marriage

---
[*]Editor, *Faith at Work* Magazine.

is built consciously and knowingly by two persons who respect each other and work at it. To weave a relationship sturdy enough to stand all the tests of life, they will need these four strands: *communication, commitment, understanding,* and *grace.*

Communication. It is surprising how little some couples know of each other when they marry. Or perhaps it is not surprising at all. We spend much of our time in putting on a good appearance — "making ourselves presentable" — and in the process hiding our real selves from others.

A famous Halloween cartoon shows three youngsters standing before an open door, shouting "trick or treat" as they remove their masks. Two of the children are pulling off ogre masks, revealing innocent cherub faces. But the third is taking off the mask of an innocent cherub only to reveal the face of an ogre. We laugh at these youngsters, but it is our world of pretense that they expose.

Especially is this true when we lose our hearts in romantic love. We want the other person to like us so we let her see us only at our best, carefully hiding our insecurities, our fears and guilt. There is something in us that wants to be known but not at the risk of "losing her." So she finds out what we really are only with great difficulty. And if she does not want to know — preferring to idealize us — she will not find out at all.

How innocent and unknowing a bride and groom can be as they repeat their vows! How much of discovery awaits them! One thing is certain: if they did not know each other well *before* marriage, they will have to come to know each other *within* the marriage, or it will fail.

Each partner must be willing to be fully known. He will come to see this sooner or later, especially if he has reason to doubt the other's love. He may put it this way: "She

When the Jitters Take Over / 95

says she loves me, but she doesn't really know me. It's obvious that what she loves is her image of me. And the only way I can be sure she loves the *real* me is to let her know me."

On the other side of this coin is our desire to know the one we love — her past experiences, her feelings, her likes and dislikes, even her problems and weaknesses. If this is not true — if we want only an idealized fantasy rather than the real person — we betray our inability to love maturely.

To know and to be known, to be accepted as we are — this is true love, the first strand in the rope of marriage.

Part of this strand is learning to talk and listen at new levels of understanding. We must communicate in times of conflict and not go off to sulk. Conflict will inevitably come. The more a relationship demands intimacy, the greater is the possibility of conflict — and true love can grow only as we face the conflicts and talk honestly about them rather than seek "peace at any price" and avoid all risks.

But we must learn to talk in the language that the other understands, and this involves listening intently. Here is a young husband who wants to say "I love you" to his bride. His way of saying it is to take her to a movie. But she doesn't get the message. "He just wants to get out of the house," she says to herself. "If he really wanted to show his love, he'd wash the dishes." And so his attempt to say "I love you" is not heard.

Commitment. A strange thing happens when a man and woman exchange marriage vows. In the common wording of the ceremony they say to each other, "I *take* thee to be my lawful wedded wife," and "I *take* thee to be my lawful wedded husband." But in reality they do not mean, "I take," so much as, "I give." The pledge into which they enter is to give themselves to each other, without reservation, and what they promise is to take responsibility for each other's happiness. The reverse wording has deep meaning, for there is no taking without giving, and no getting for oneself without giving to the other.

Many a marriage begins immaturely. Just as couples enter into marriage without knowing each other well, so they may be more engrossed in what they are going to get from the relationship than what they intend to give to it. After the newness has worn off and they do not find themselves getting all they expected, disillusionment sets in.

The real test of the relationship comes when a partner discovers that his mate does not come up to all his expectations (and who does?), nor can she meet all his personal needs (and who can?). If his idea of marriage was unrealistic, he is likely to decide that he made a mistake and married the wrong girl. His solution then will be to get out of a bad situation and start the search once more for "the right woman."

The problem may not be that he married the wrong woman, but that he is the wrong man. Very likely he can achieve happiness in marriage if he will recognize his delusions and selfishness and make a new start, not by getting out but by staying in.

Can he do this? It will depend on his willingness to weave the strand of commitment into the rope of his marriage. He said, "Until death us do part." Did he mean it?

Commitment to the permanence of marriage is a prerequisite for facing its conflicts and resolving them. Make room in your mind for the reservation, "I can get out of this if I want to," and you undercut the determination that is necessary to struggle through the reassessments and realignments of responsibility, and to reach understanding.

In almost every tangled marriage at least one of the

When the Jitters Take Over / 97

partners is shirking his responsibility but loudly asserting his rights. Rights and responsibilities are inseparable. Rights always bring responsibilities, and only responsible people can claim any rights.

Therefore commitment is a strand that must be woven into the rope. Even a marriage that is foundering — that began in a flush of excitement but bogged down into apathy or cold war — can be redeemed. If the partners will face themselves, more realistically now, and recommit themselves to their responsibilities, they can begin all over and build a growing and ever more satisfying relationship.

Understanding. Another strand is needed for the fulfillment of a marriage. A couple may communicate freely and be sincerely committed to each other, and yet fail through lack of knowledge of the demands marriage makes of them.

Do they understand that marriage cannot be an end in itself, but that they need to have a goal "above and beyond" to which their marriage is committed? If they have been nursed on the philosophy of our time — that eternal values are bankrupt and that all one can be sure of is human love — they are likely to fall in love with love and marry simply to be married, rather than to dedicate their marriage to the goal of serving God and people.

Do they understand the roles of husband and wife, of father and mother? Are they mature enough to function freely in their roles, or did he marry unconsciously searching for a mother to take care of him, or she a father to dominate her? If so, they will expect the wrong things from their partners and give the wrong things themselves.

Do they understand and agree on the value of money and material possessions, on cultural and intellectual values, on personal standards, and on the disciplines with which they will surround their children?

What sources of insight are available to them? First of all, honesty will make them realistic about themselves and others. Knowledge of their family backgrounds will prepare them for possible conflicts in values. When two young people marry, in reality two families are joined together, and if there are great differences — material, social, religious, racial — the obstacles may be enormous. Interaction with those who have gone on before can be helpful, as can reading books that explain the dynamics and possible pitfalls of marriage. Professional help, when it is available — sound therapy and counseling, either individually or in groups — can solve difficult problems and add new dimensions to marriage.

My wife and I had been married more than ten years before we discovered the depths of sharing that we were missing, and we learned it only through a crisis. One of our children developed asthma. The antigen our physician prescribed brought relief but no solution. So we went at last — pride notwithstanding — to a marriage counselor. He observed and tested our child and then announced, "There's nothing wrong with *him,* but you two aren't communicating." We admitted then, openly, what we had known subconsciously, and sought the help both of professional counselors and Christian friends. As we were able to express ourselves we grew in love and trust and our child's asthma disappeared. While all of this was going on we appeared outwardly to many of our friends to be "the ideal family," but little did they know the blind spots in our self-understanding nor the growth pains that accompanied our forward progress.

Grace. What has been said so far presupposes a fourth strand in the rope of marriage: this strand is the grace of

When the Jitters Take Over / 99

God, which gives hope of achieving wonderful new possibilities in marriage.

There is grace for every failure — forgiveness from God so complete that we can forgive each other and even ourselves, and begin again.

Colleen Townsend Evans tells of a friend who was caught by her husband in an indiscreet act. She loved her husband and was full of remorse, and her husband loved her, but together they agreed that there was nothing to do but be divorced. Their religious faith knew nothing of forgiveness, so they tearfully discussed plans for separation. But as they did so, their eyes fell on a book Colleen had loaned them, unopened until now, a volume of sermons by Peter Marshall. They picked it up and it fell open to a sermon on Jesus and "the woman taken in adultery." They read it together and discovered that God is forgiving. Excitedly they called Colleen and asked to talk to her, and that night in Colleen's kitchen they accepted God's forgiveness in Christ and began a whole new life together.

There is grace for weaklings, grace that puts courage into the timid and enables them to take new steps, face responsibility, and work their way through challenges and change. Another name for this grace is the Holy Spirit, God present with His people.

And, finally, there is grace to love. Love's true source is outside ourselves in the One who made us. The love that originates in us is selfish and possessive, but the love that comes from God enables us to give ourselves unselfishly and to set people free to grow into their full potential.

I remember how startled I was to discover, after marriage, that I did not have the capacity to love my wife adequately. I had thought I was quite a "lover" and that my only problem was to find the right object for my love.

I found the right wife and married her, only to discover how selfish and incapable I was of mature love.

But this discovery set us both free, for in it I also found that we must not expect from each other what is not in our power to give. No human being can fully meet the needs of another. A true marriage exists only in God, in whom there is love sufficient to meet every need and to realize every potential.

IV. That Fourth Dimension

IV. That Fourth Dimension

A Question of Surrender

The baby was dead, and for Sherman and Susan it was a time of terror and testing. Then, in a little-used book, they began to find answers for their unanswerable questions.

A few years ago, I walked away from twenty-five years of experience in industry, and, with my family, took a sabbatical of five months. We could not really afford this, but there was never any doubt that the means would be provided, once we were sure we were moving forward as God directed.

To give up all connections with a business that had been our means of support for a quarter of a century, to do nothing by way of earning daily bread for five months — and then to move into an area of work that was not only somewhat strange, but also full of uncertainty regarding financial returns — would have been virtually impossible under "normal" circumstances. But I had been prepared by an important lesson that came early in my Christian experience. This was the lesson of *surrender*.

To many people this word denotes weakness, but to me it is one of the most strength-demanding terms in the language. This is how I came to learn this lesson.

One evening some years ago I walked into the bedroom where our first child, then five months old, lay sleeping. He was an active boy, so healthy and robust that I could easily see him as a powerful college full-back in a few years. But the minute I looked at him that night I knew he was dead. One minute a perfectly healthy son; the next, a lifeless body.

How hard it is to know there is a God and try to justify such a tragedy. There had been no accident — no sign of struggle — just a sleep that did not end.

Though my wife Susan and I were nominal Christians, we were unprepared spiritually for such an occurrence. Restless nights followed, and sometimes I became aware in the small hours of the morning that Susan was gone, and I knew she was driving aimlessly through deserted streets, trying to find an answer she could accept.

At such times nothing fits. Months go by and you try to adjust to life and to old associations, but these are now strained. No one seems to know what to say or do.

Our marriage had only just begun, and it was truly founded on a deep and abiding love, but how could we face the future with such an experience darkening our dreams? How could we dare to have another child and bear to leave him alone even for a moment?

Several months later, when we were expecting the next child, Susan was both physically sick and very, very frightened. We had moved to a new city and there was no one to turn to for help. Every morning I had to leave Susan to face hours of misery all alone. It was hell for her, and hell for me to leave her.

One morning she asked me to read something from the Bible, which lay almost unused on the bedside table. I read a psalm. Susan seemed to withstand the hours of darkness with some comfort that day. The next morning I read another psalm, and she began to respond to this new-found therapy.

That Fourth Dimension / 105

Little by little, out of the blackness of despair, our search for comfort in the Word of God became the most wonderful and fruitful time of our day. We started to pray, though at first we were shy and our prayers together were stumbling. Somehow, we came to realize that God alone has control of the realm beyond human love. As we became aware that only He could guide the really important events of our existence, we surrendered ourselves to Him. Together, we tried to give Him every phase of our lives in complete relinquishment.

At first, fifteen minutes of prayer and Bible study seemed a long time, but over the years this time together has grown into a wonderful bond. Even when I am traveling, we are together by uniting our spirits in God's Spirit across the miles. And today an hour isn't enough.

My day is created during this early morning hour. Whatever the day may bring, its problems are solved before they actually find expression. Each day we try to surrender ourselves to God, for we know that the greatest thing that can happen is for His will to be accomplished. Of course, there are days when we fail to find this pattern, because self and pride get in the way, but we continue to grow toward the goal of complete acceptance of His will.

After several years another time of testing came. We had told God we would go anywhere or do anything He might ask. We felt a clear sense of direction to get away from the hubbub of the world for an extended time of quiet and prayer. After five months, we returned to the world of industry, and the way opened for me to become a free-lance consultant to management. During the five months, other opportunities had arisen which seemed attractive, as they involved a more direct service in "God's work." But again, surrender of the matter closed the wrong doors and opened the right ones.

Since beginning this work I have never solicited assignments. I leave the supply up to God, and requests for my services come in with sufficient regularity to afford utilization of all my time. All along the route there are opportunities to speak of what God has done for us, and these fit right into my business schedule.

The lesson of surrender, however, will not stand alone for long. Soon we found other important lessons were needed for our growth. In almost every situation, we began to see the gift of faith becoming a necessary adjunct to relinquishment. Some of the situations we face involve others, so that our surrender of them would be presumptuous, except for the gift of faith.

For example, one time when I was managing a manufacturing plant, a supervisor who worked for me was doing an inadequate job. In spite of all the help given by the staff and me, he just wasn't able to bring his department into line. He'd been warned that he would be replaced unless his work improved within a reasonable length of time. But nothing worked, so I asked him to come to my office, planning to discharge him.

At my usual time of prayer that morning, I asked God to direct me in what I said to this man. The question popped into my mind, "Have you done all you can for him?" I felt I had, and said so, but the question persisted.

I asked the Lord what I could do that I had not already done. This led to my praying in a very specific way for the man. I felt directed to set aside an additional fifteen minutes each morning to pray for him in his work. So instead of discharging him that day, I told him what had happened, and said I would be praying for him through another thirty-day period. In less than three weeks a marvelous change came into his department. As far as I know that man is still working for the same company.

I rarely know where I will be more than a week ahead, but my wife and I have learned not to fear. Often assignments come which I would not otherwise accept, because I don't feel qualified to solve their particular problems, but trusting in God I have always found that He supplies the necessary resources. It's wonderful to watch His plan unfold each day, if we just stay out of the way.

Typical

> *Ginny and Cal had "a selfish religion — it made us feel good for an hour every Sunday morning." Then insurmountable problems arose, and they had to grow up.*

The Coopers, Ginny and Cal, call themselves "a typical young couple," and they have a nice home, a good income, and a healthy baby girl. Not long ago they became members of W_____ Church and started going regularly to services there; but, Mrs. Cooper says, "Ours was a selfish religion — it made us feel good for an hour every Sunday morning. We never gave a thought to a personal God."

A few months later something happened. Ginny starts at the beginning and tells the story:

"My parents were divorced when I was quite young, and I grew up feeling insecure and different. I spent much of my young life in tears because I felt unloved. When I met new people I was apt to assume an insincere air in an effort to impress them. I distrusted almost everyone.

"I met Cal while I was attending college. In him, I

thought, was the security I longed for; here was someone I loved who truly loved me. I thrived on our relationship during courting days, and we were married when I finished school.

"Although we loved each other very much, problems soon arose and some of them seemed insurmountable. Many a miserable day was spent as we became increasingly conscious that solutions were evading us.

"Soon after our daughter was born the young assistant minister at our church called on me. I didn't know him or why he had come, but we chatted for a while and before I realized what I was saying I told him I was looking for 'a day-to-day relationship with God.' The words surprised me, but not the visitor. He understood, and invited us to visit a fellowship group. There, happy surprise, we found people like ourselves, except that they were finding how to live daily with God.

"We joined this group and, as we saw how to give our own lives over, God began to work in us. He taught us how to pray together and how to ask for, and receive, guidance about problems — and also how to make decisions. Most important, after a while, He helped us to realize that we were nothing without Him and His love.

"I especially needed forgiveness — forgiveness for my parents, for I found that I held deep resentments toward them and blamed them for my years of unhappiness. Forgiveness also for myself, for I had long hated myself for being the kind of person I was.

"Cal and I have had some wonderful experiences together. One day I was angry with him because he had been late, avoidably. That night we skipped prayers together, but in my own prayers I knew (although I didn't understand why) that God continued to love Cal anyway, what-

That Fourth Dimension / 109

ever his faults. I asked God if He wouldn't let me borrow some of that love. The next morning there were no signs of anger, no long 'I'm sorries,' but just a home filled with God's love."

Cal takes up the story:

"Last May we decided we should own our own home. Realizing that perhaps we weren't to have a house right then, we prayed that God would go with us as we looked; that if there was a house available He would either make the way clear or put blocks in our way.

"We looked at several places and finally found a house that appeared to fit all our requirements and needs. It was a beautiful new house set in a perfectly landscaped plot. Ginny and I felt that surely this must be the place for us, and in our nightly prayer time again asked God to guide us. The very next morning I began to make arrangements to buy, but there were blocks — problems at the bank, about the location, the construction, and several other things. After one day of this we felt that God had made His wishes known. We forgot about that house.

"Our search went on and again we found a place we both liked. This time my wife had some misgivings, so on our next visit we decided to stop and pray right there in the middle of the unplastered living room and ask God to make known His plans to us. Ginny was almost immediately convinced that this *was* to be our new home, and we both felt that we had been given the signal to go ahead. We signed the contracts within the week."

Cal explains that he does not mean to equate guidance and easy progress. Two weeks before occupancy a shortage of proper tiling appeared. A week later trouble threatened from a government angle. But "God's guidance was evident," Cal concludes, "in every phase of that house. Nations may have their guided missiles, but we have our *guided* home."

Out of Bitterness

Peter and Enid were certain God was punishing them. Perhaps if they adopted a baby they could get their marriage back on an even keel. . . .

After our son Kevin was born we wanted very much to have other children, but over the years there were indications that this was not to be. After a great deal of medical care, however, we discovered to our great joy that we were going to have another baby.

Three weeks before the child was to be born X-rays revealed that it could not be born alive. During those weeks we sank into deep despair, railing against fate, the church, our minister — until we were blaming God one minute and doubting His existence the next.

The baby girl was stillborn, and for the next month we lived in a state of depression and resentment. When the minister came to visit us we poured out our bitterness in a torrent of unkind remarks. We couldn't understand why God was punishing us this way.

At last we decided to look into the question of adoption and were invited to a meeting with other prospective adoptive parents. Arriving too early for the meeting, we decided to wander through a book store.

We had selected a new cookbook and were on our way to the counter when too little boys wrestling in the aisle forced us to step aside. One of us caught a glimpse of the book, *The Power of Positive Thinking*, by Norman Vincent Peale, and for some reason we bought it instead of the cookbook.

That Fourth Dimension / 111

After the meeting that day we were sitting at the kitchen table looking at the new book. We began to read it together, and after we'd gone through a few pages a most unusual thing happened. Without conscious thought we rose from the table, got down on our knees, and began to pray aloud together. It was the first time we had done such a thing in all the years of our married life.

What happened as we prayed together is impossible to describe. It was as if the Lord walked in and took over in the space of a few minutes. We felt as if we were no longer ourselves, but two new and different persons.

The results of this encounter with Christ were immediate. We stopped feeling sorry for ourselves, and felt a peace and joy we had never known before. Later we saw that we had never before given the Lord any real place in our lives. Church attendance was just "the thing to do." We ran our own lives and thought we were doing a good job of it until something came along that we couldn't handle. What had we been living for? What had been our aims and purposes? Unconsciously we had been seeking to know God, but had never seen who He was.

Since giving our lives to Him, we have found many selfish areas in ourselves, and we see that it is a day-by-day "giving over" that must be done; that Jesus continually points out sins and weaknesses, but also shows the way and gives the strength for necessary changes.

Each of us has found new avenues for service. Peter is in Sunday school work, an evening study group, and a noon-hour men's gathering. He is trying to practice the principles of Christianity in his work, and this has proved to be the most challenging matter of all.

Enid has found a place in the church choir, and in a similar evening fellowship group, and she is now a frequent visitor to the local old people's home. Together we are discovering how we can be of help to others through a simple sharing of our experiences and failures. We also find that Christ gives direction as we do our best to encourage others.

Last May a little girl, four months old, came to live with us. Catherine is a constant reminder to us of God's love, and we feel a sense of completion and happiness as a family. While we regret the time wasted in the past, our foremost feeling today is one of gratitude for the new depth in our love for each other, for our families, and for other people.

"This Has Me Licked!"

Sally's mother-in-law was impossible. There was no question about it: the whole family agreed. And now she was coming for an extended visit. . . .

For most things Sally had an answer, but not for this. "This has me licked!" she cried in despair.

She had been happily married many years, had raised her children successfully, and had met the problems of life with faith and fortitude. But for this problem she could find no answer.

In fact the whole family was baffled. They had come to look upon it as "just one of those things," something to be endured because it was beyond solution. They had pushed this relationship into the "defeat" compartment, for it involved a grandmother who wanted only her own way, who refused all reasonable solutions to problems and all offers of love. They had come to accept the fact that she was beyond reach, and the best thing was to stay as far away from her as possible. The "mother-in-law problem" can be more than a laughing matter!

That Fourth Dimension / 113

Two years ago Sally became an active member of a prayer group, and entered into a period of rapid spiritual growth. Although she had been a lifelong Christian, acceptance of Christ and life in the Holy Spirit were not *practical* realities. Now she was discovering for herself what the New Testament Christians wrote about.

Then into this good life came her mother-in-law's announcement — she was arriving for an extended visit at Christmastime. Of all times this was the worst! It meant that the happy days to which the family looked forward would be spoiled, as they always were when Grandmother came to visit.

This time, however, there was a difference. Instead of complaining, Sally prayed about the problem in a new way she had learned in the prayer group: "Lord, I can't love her. You know I have tried and how she has refused my love. But I believe that *You* love her, as You love me, with Your patient, divine, redemptive love. Therefore, I surrender myself and my relationship with her to You. Cleanse me from every unloving feeling toward her. And, when she comes to our house, love her through me. I give myself to You so that I can be Your way of reaching her with Your love."

Later Sally told about her mother-in-law's visit, and this time it was a different story. She herself felt free of strain and apprehension. Christ *did* love the older woman through her, and the impossible person *was* different. Somehow the love of Christ reached her and altered her nature, at least a little, for she let herself be helped and loved as never before.

The whole family was aware of the difference. Sally knew that the answer started in her own changed attitude, and she was grateful for this discovery. She was learning that this is the way Christ intends His people to use the power of His presence in every situation.

"Adequate" — for What?

> *Elaine felt guilty about her nagging discontent. Steve didn't feel guilty about anything; he was too busy trying to maintain the status quo, which "consisted in no small part of mixing drinks and listening to records."*

Steve and Elaine Linder came to Texas from Ohio, by way of Washington, D.C. Both had been raised in church but had left it in their teenage years and didn't return until they found St. S_____'s a dozen years ago.

By this time Elaine, who outwardly seemed to have everything necessary for happiness, was thoroughly disillusioned. Education hadn't brought happiness, nor had marriage, though it was supposed to erase automatically all self-doubt and inadequacy. Among her friends Elaine began to see increasing failures — divorce, alcoholism, mental breakdown — and she was frightened. Life was letting her down, and she wondered if she and Steve would be spared.

This is how Steve describes the early years of his and Elaine's marriage:

"We were what you might call a 'good' family. There were strong ties between parents, a willingness to make sacrifices (within limits), loyalty to and pride in the family unit, the blessings of good health and education and financial security, and a sincere desire to do 'the right thing' in all circumstances.

"But we were a family without faith. In all the years of

That Fourth Dimension / 115

our marriage we had not prayed, and the subject of going to church never came up.

"We had some lofty and noble ideas about marriage, during the early years, and vague notions of 'perfection.' We believed strongly in education and in the value of intelligent judgment for solving problems. Our highest goals could be characterized as strongly humanistic.

"Our first two children were born, but even amid the activities of parenthood each of us felt that something was wrong. Despite our advantages, life was not a joyful experience. With all our good intentions we were never satisfied. The symptoms of the illness went all but unrecognized: a love for our children that was selfish and possessive, a great deal of effort spent in the pursuit of pleasure, and a reliance on the security of home and family above all other considerations.

"Our reactions to this nagging discontent were quite opposite. Elaine felt guilty and blamed herself, while constantly seeking explanations and solutions. I didn't feel guilty about anything. I was primarily concerned with maintaining the status quo, wanting only to be left alone. And the status quo consisted in no small part of mixing drinks and listening to records!

"This pattern might have gone on indefinitely had my wife's searching not led her into contact with a strong and active church where people seemed to know about recognizing and solving problems. . . ."

The move to Texas had been a radical one, into a whole new atmosphere. For one thing, everyone seemed to go to church. When a new acquaintance invited Elaine to attend St. S_____'s, she went purely out of curiosity. She fumbled through the order of service, but when the sermon started she sat bolt upright. "He talked like a machine gun," she recalls, "and it was all about me. I wondered who had tipped him off that I was there."

God has a plan for one's life, the preacher insisted, and He will communicate it day by day if we listen. On the way home, Elaine said to her friend, "It's all right for him to talk that way; he's a priest. But I don't think it would work for me. Do you?"

"Yes, I do," was the straightforward reply.

The next day Elaine made her first tentative experiment at prayer since childhood. She felt foolish getting down on her knees beside the bed, and didn't know if anyone even heard her plea for help. But she went through the ritual again the next day, and the third day found herself repeating a simple prayer whenever she felt anxiety or pressure.

A month later, as she was washing luncheon dishes and feeling the weight of the world on her shoulders, she repeated the prayer, and, as she tells it, "was filled with the love of God from head to toe. I was so excited that I started out the back door to tell someone — anyone — that I had found God. But that didn't seem wise, on second thought, so I waited to tell Steve when he came home from work. I felt sure he would laugh in my face, but he didn't. He wanted to know all about it."

With the experience of God's love came a sense of sin — an unacceptable word until now — and an equal sense of God's acceptance which made it possible for Elaine, for the first time, to accept herself. She thanked God for this and asked Him what to do next. The answer was clear: Join the church and get to work. So she entered the confirmation class and asked the rector to give her a job.

Meanwhile she reported everything to Steve, who listened attentively but showed no inclination to follow her lead. As she prayed about Steve, God told her to stop talk-

That Fourth Dimension / 117

ing — and to quit leaving those pamphlets around for him to read. When she obeyed, Steve's curiosity began to get the best of him.

Steve is quiet and reserved. Behind his placid exterior, it is easy to envisage a kindly, sweet man. But Steve says that actually he was smug and contented with himself, and extremely critical of others.

Proud of his background, his achievements in business, and his family (in spite of his inner alienation), he felt no need for outside help. He was repelled when Elaine invited him to meetings at church called "The Witnessing Fellowship of Need." *Witnessing* and *fellowship* were bad words and needs were things other people had — not Steve.

"But when Elaine clammed up on me," he admits, "I had to find out for myself what was going on. But I didn't participate. I just sat and listened."

At last Steve was softened up to the point where he was willing to attend confirmation classes. There he heard laymen speak briefly about their faith, and he was overwhelmed. Each week a different layman spoke. "They came in all sizes, shapes, and ages," he recalls, "but they had one thing in common. They spoke of God without embarrassment, and told of His love for them and how they were trying to fulfill His plan. They seemed to be busy, effective people, well disciplined, while I was totally undisciplined. I looked forward to each meeting and as time went on I wanted to be like these people. By the time I was confirmed I had committed my life to the Lord.

"Through this church we heard for the first time that God is deeply concerned with us as individuals, and wants our concern in return. We found that people really do commit themselves to God on a day-to-day basis. We saw the requirements, disciplines, and results of a Christian life, and ultimately we came to experience some of these same things ourselves.

"The essential difference this had made in our life is that we as parents have the certain knowledge that our strength and purpose do not rest on the family, a good name, education, 'togetherness,' or any other thing, worthy as these may be. They rest only on God as revealed in Christ. We now recognize that our failures — and there are many — are not pleasing to God, but that they need not weigh us down. We have been given a new perspective.

"The knowledge that all good things come from God and not from our own efforts makes us grateful for what we have and what we get. We sense that what we actually deserve is far less than what we have been given.

"We see that to love children is not to possess them. Our role as parents is one of stewardship. This understanding makes it possible for us to let our children be themselves as individuals, and it also enables us to administer discipline without apology. Our responsibility as parents is deeper than we once understood it to be, but we are no longer anxious about it.

"We have lost the compulsion to make long-range plans, which in our case often constituted an attempt to order our own future. Now we see that life's opportunities are primarily *today's*.

"We have seen that we need to help and be helped by others. The self-sufficient family we once tried to be simply does not exist.

"Most important, God is now at the center of our lives. We have the certain knowledge that He will show us what to do, if we will only follow."

If You Want to Change the World

Gordon and Frances were young and idealistic. They had a "world view." But how were they to go about righting the wrongs which they saw all about them?

Gordon says: Idealists want to change the world, to make it a better place. Though I considered myself an idealist, I had no idea how to go about this until I met people who were being changed themselves.

During my navy years I was stationed at Alameda Air Force Base in California, dividing my free time between the "bar and burlycue" circuit, intellectual stimulation at the University of California, and religious interests. Some friends took me to a place called the Port of Call, a club for young people run in connection with an evangelical church — the kind where they have "altar calls." One night, out of curiosity, I answered the call myself. I was taken into a back room and asked if I wanted to give my life to Christ, or something like that. I was trapped: these people were friends, and I couldn't just walk out. Two boys were on their knees praying for me, and I suddenly felt guilty and hypocritical. At that moment and in the weeks that followed I became aware of my own dishonesty. I was leading a double life.

My emotions were touched, and I started to think about Jesus. I believed in God, and could see Jesus as an historical figure, but some of my friends talked about "knowing Him as a person." This concept left me cold, yet one night as I lay in my bunk thinking about all this, something powerful happened to me. Suddenly I saw Jesus in a new way — as the focal point of history. I saw Him both as an eternal spirit and as an immediate presence. I saw Him as *intimate* and as *ultimate*.

Thinking this over further, I decided to declare myself a Christian. I told my navy buddies and friends at the Port of Call. With one close friend in particular I had many conversations, and one night I asked him if he wanted to give his life to Christ. He broke down and cried, and seemed to be completely shattered. This alarmed me and squelched any further attempts at witnessing.

When I got home to New Jersey I still wanted to tell people about my faith, but was afraid of looking ridiculous. I wasn't growing, and as time passed my faith became more nostalgic than meaningful. Not until I met Frances and got in touch with a fellowship group were the sparks kindled again.

Frances says: I was very much like Gordon, wanting my life to have significance. As a teacher I was full of idealism, sure that I could make the world a little better.

My school was in an underprivileged neighborhood, and I spent a lot of time with "problem children" among them one who had been badly neglected, unloved by his parents, in and out of orphanages. Tommy had been in school three years before it was discovered that he was very deaf, and as a result his behavior was terrible.

With all the attention I gave him, he began to read well. But the next year, with a different teacher, he went backward. I saw that Tommy was just like the other children — you could give him new clothes, correct his hearing, teach him how to read, *but you could not change his basic human nature*.

About this time my mother had a deep religious experience that really showed in her disposition and in her relationships with the family. I began to wonder if there

That Fourth Dimension

was something in Christianity I had missed. It interested me that Mother had a personal faith and relationship with God. On the sly I read some of her books, but at the same time what I showed the world was the gay, frivolous Southern belle, devoted to pretty clothes, dates, and having a ball.

Eventually I came to New York hoping that if I got away from the conventions of home I could search for the meaning of life and find some real values for myself. Even then, in my early twenties, I had seen several of my friends' marriages end in divorce. These were people who had tried to find ultimate happiness in each other. I had also decided that wealth did not bring happiness, for I had known several people of considerable wealth who were miserable.

Years before I had discarded church groups, but through a peculiar set of circumstances I found myself one night at a young adults' meeting at a downtown church. In this group were people who were attractive, well-educated, and personable. Curiosity got me into a small group designed for "seekers." For months I attended without saying a word, terrified of becoming involved. It was exciting, however, to hear how different ones were trying experiments in faith.

Experimentation appealed to me because it didn't mean total involvement. I started to pray for my boss, who didn't like me and whom I resented. As I prayed, it became clear to me that Charlie was miserable in his job — a fact I hadn't seen before. Then he started to smile in the morning and say hello. We became friends. And then Charlie got a better job with another company!

Then I started to pray for a girl in the office whom no one liked, and though we never became bosom pals, she and I ended up appreciating each other. She stopped criticizing me and her whole attitude changed.

These and other incidents convinced me that there was something in prayer, and I reported these things in the group meetings, which meant I was getting involved. Bubbling over with excitement, I spilled all this out to Gordon the first time we met. As we dated I continued to talk about "the group" and all the wonderful things that were beginning to happen.

Then I fell in love with Gordon, though he told me frankly I was not the only girl he was dating. Ridiculous as it sounds, this situation created my first real sense of need. I had something to pray about now! My whole commitment of my life to God involved this issue, for I thought if I didn't get Gordon life was going to be pretty drab. When I shared this problem with others, it was suggested that God's plan for my life might not include Gordon, but whatever His plan was it was the highest good for me. Somehow I understood that I was putting my desire for Gordon ahead of my desire to serve God. One morning I was tidying up the apartment, feeling vaguely unclean, as if there was something I needed to do and hadn't done. I put down the vacuum cleaner, sat on the couch, and said, "Oh, Lord! Take it! Take the whole thing! I don't know if You want me to marry Gordon, but even if You want me to be an old maid it will be a more exciting life than anything I could dream up for myself."

What a release! When I got free about my feeling for Gordon, naturally I changed toward him. Now he could see in me not just a theology but a faith that really worked.

Our relationship had reached an impasse, and if we were to break up I wanted it to be on good terms, without misunderstanding or bitterness. I suggested that we pray together. Afterwards there seemed to be a third dimension

That Fourth Dimension / 123

in our relationship. We began to understand and communicate with each other as never before.

Gordon resumes: It startled me when Frances asked me to pray aloud with her. My feeling was that a person should commune with God in silence. So while Frances knelt and prayed I simply added, "For Christ's sake, Amen." This got us into a big discussion of what Christ meant to us. The result was that Frances started to be more concrete and specific, and I myself, having prayed aloud with another person, felt a great deal more free.

In spite of my idealism, I'd never given myself wholly to a project or idea, nor thought in terms of a spiritual dynamic. I got this new challenge through contacts with Frances and the fellowship at her church. Here were people who would encourage me, check up on me, pray with me — each one giving a part of the truth to others as God guided him. Here was a focus for my idealism, for here were people changing before my very eyes, and with every person made new in Christ the world changed a bit, too.

I saw things that had to be straightened out in my life, if I wanted honestly to be a part of this thing. I wasn't much of a rounder — my life was more wasted than wicked — but there were things that required definite action. This led to the discovery that Christ could make the difference not only for those who were desperate, but also for those who seemed to do all right in their own strength.

Throughout our engagement, Frances and I prayed together about our life, for we wanted not just a routine marriage but one in which Christ would have supreme importance. Part of the original commitment of our marriage was that we wanted to share the love God had given us with other people. So we have always tried to share freely of whatever we have found, whether a deep experience or something quite insignificant.

For example, at a weekend conference in Massachusetts, we became friends with a young couple, Fred and Penny. They weren't much interested in the conference, but chauffeured us around from place to place. Right away the four of us hit it off — we just had fun together. They decided to go to some of the meetings, and on Saturday night in the car, we asked Fred what he thought of them.

Suddenly he opened up and told us that things weren't going well for Penny and him; they were even thinking about divorce. After he'd finished, the three of us prayed together about this situation. We suggested that when he got home he pray with Penny, and unknown to us this was a conviction that had been growing in *her* mind all through the weekend. When Fred asked his wife to pray with him, she nearly collapsed in surprise.

Such things happen not through design, but only because we try to be open to God's leading. With Fred and Penny we weren't "evangelizing"; we had nothing in mind but to be friends. God led them to begin again that weekend, and this triggered a recommitment of *our* marriage to Him.

Nothing compares with the excitement of seeing the love of God in action, transforming the lives of people. You find it happening in your own life, and it's the greatest adventure you can ever know. Do you want to change the world? Of course you can, if you begin at the beginning and let God change *you*.

V. Children: Complication or Compensation?

V. Children: Complication or Compensation?

Glad We Get Along

It warmed Ken's heart — and raised his eyebrows — to hear his daughter's estimate of their life as a family. For what were their outstanding accomplishments?

"All I can say is I'm certainly glad we get along together in *our* family," exclaimed eighteen-year-old Karen as we drove home from Vacation Bible School. My eyebrows went up and she grinned, "*Fairly* well, anyhow!" Then she made a friendly grimace in the direction of her brother Max, age ten, who sat between us in the front seat.

We'd been talking about family relations, especially as they applied to behavior problems that kept cropping up in the school. Karen, a kindergarten helper, was roiled, and Max was anything but pleased at having to attend a Bible school where wildness seemed to be the order of the day.

We live in an inner-city area where there is much disorganization of life and a concentration of human woe. Just the night before I had been involved in the wild anger of a mother and the bitter despair of a father, and had seen with sorrow the round-eyed stillness of three little children as they watched the battle.

Though I lifted my eyebrows to tease Karen, her remark gave me a sense of real gratitude. Ours is a "typical" home, with all-too-human parents who often fail, but in spite of this it is a home where mistakes and inadequacies are dealt with in the light of commitment to Christ.

Our family is typical also in that we can boast of no outstanding accomplishments. We have tried many plans for family worship, for example, without ever arriving at one which "worked" for any length of time. Some of these plans served admirably for the time being. At one point we tried periods of silence and listening prayer, with pencils and notebooks, and at this time our most reticent child found it possible to "hear" God speak to him regarding personal faults.

Then we also tried family worship of a more formal nature, praying aloud and singing around the piano. At another point we met early in the morning and read to each other from *The Pilgrim's Progress*.

I have been prone to dwell on the things we were *not* seeming to accomplish, not getting across to the kids, from simple things such as good table manners to important ones like facing hardship with spirit and courage. At times I am likely to brood not only about apparent family failures but also about professional inadequacy, but when this happens I see again that there is nothing to do but turn the whole business over to God and let Him deal with it. Always, when I reach this point, life picks up again with a time of creative accomplishment.

Our children are used to family decisions made in prayer. I remember the time our old car came to "the end of the road" with a case of burnt-out bearings. Almost at once we found an excellent, serviceable car, reasonably priced, but our sons, teenage Dan and young Max, did not appreciate this timely solution. To them, a ten-year-old car might as well have been Noah's Ark.

Children: Complication or Compensation? / 129

Finally we sat down together to face the decision, just before a summer trip. After free expression of opinions and ideas, we prayed for light on this matter. Max was genuinely fearful that if it were left up to God, it would be the ten-year-old model. But after prayer he did not complain, even when it seemed clear that the thing to do was patch up the old car and hope for the best. We compensated somewhat by installing new seat-covers.

Early in our married life my wife and I discovered that there is a difference between trying to guide God's hand and letting Him make the decisions. I was just beginning to pay attention to deep inner faults that, like blisters on the heel, were slowing me down.

We came in touch with people to whom God was more real than He was to us, and we both began to see more clearly what God wanted us to do. We became honest with each other, and as barriers went down we began a life of more conscious faith and teamwork in home and church. It is this kind of relationship that we have tried to establish with each of our children.

Much fault remains, but we do know how to acknowledge mistakes, and this results in openness with each other and freedom in the home. Life's hectic moments are balanced with times of deep spiritual communication.

We have found open hospitality to be a tremendous boon. Many people have lived with us over the years, some for short periods of time and some for months. Each has brought something fresh and vital into the family atmosphere. At the moment our home is full of teenagers, our own and others. They are "stretchers" for us at times, but we are learning a lot, and loving it.

Asthma and an Answer

In other people's children, of course, Nan's ailments could have been attributed to emotional factors. But Nan's mother couldn't see where she had missed the boat.

Last autumn my daughter Nan, six years old, had her first attack of asthma. She had outgrown eczema at four and graduated to hay fever at five. What's more, she is also a thumb-sucker.

I believe that all these things in *other people's* children are caused by emotional factors, but I honestly couldn't see where we had missed the boat with Nan. In general she is a well-balanced little girl. She makes friends of all ages without trouble, gets good marks in school, gets into her share of devilment, and rules our home with a benevolent despotism that is both amusing and annoying. Whenever I want my husband to do something around the house, I sic Nan on him.

Since her allergies were not constant, I didn't spend much time wondering about causes. But when I watched and heard her fighting for breath during the asthma attack, I knew the time had come to do more. First Nan and I prayed. We asked God to relieve her, but He didn't. (I had many unkind thoughts as a result of that, which is another story entirely.)

Then I asked God to show me what was wrong with my relationship with Nan. First He reminded me of the time a few years ago when I went to a special study-class during Lent. This took another night a week away from home and Nan's thumb-sucking increased fifty per cent.

God also brought to mind that recently Nan had been

Children: Complication or Compensation? / 131

very insistent that I tuck her in at night, even though her dad had already done the job.

I began to think He wanted me to give up some of my activities and stay home more, but I couldn't figure where to use the axe. For a few days that was all He gave me to chew on, and chew I did until I became sick and tired of the whole mess.

Friday night we met with our regular weekly fellowship group, and I threw out the subject, with some disgust, saying I wanted to know God's will for me, but wondered why He couldn't make Himself a little clearer. Then one of our friends began asking questions such as, "Why is bedtime so important?" As I thought about the answers, *the* answer presented itself.

I have always had a fundamental feeling that I really have the right to keep a part of myself and my time to do with as I please. I have been willing to give a generous percentage of time, talent, and money to God, my husband, and my children, but surely — I've thought — they can't demand every bit of me.

My day is filled with children — four of them — and housework. It is also filled with prayer, praise, thanks, and rejoicing for the wonderful life God has given us. As I find time I try to increase my knowledge. That night I remembered a book by Elton Trueblood in which he says, "We are made to be spent." *My evenings are quite often spent in doing the Lord's work, most of it joyfully,* I thought. *When I have a free evening I can't see any reason why it should be disturbed by children to whom I have already given so much of my time and attention.*

And I realized that, while privacy was not essentially bad, what was wrong was the feeling behind it — a wall of self which said, "Everyone halt here. I have done as much as

I intend to do." Motherhood is willy-nilly a twenty-four-hour job, and discipleship requires a complete willingness to do and be anything God asks.

What was God's action in this incident? He showed me something about myself that I had seen before, but "through a glass darkly." He brought me face to face with the results of what I was. My reaction was a willingness to see what God had to say to me, knowing that it probably wouldn't be pretty, and give to Him whatever was the block and ask Him to change me.

That night I asked God to forgive me and to take away my reluctance to be a full-time mother. He did. Nan's symptoms disappeared without waiting for the first good frost. Now I am seeing my children with new eyes and increased understanding. The wall between us is beginning to evaporate.

One more thing: at the time, I thought the disappearance of Nan's illness took place because of the eradication of the wall between us. This isn't true. It only depended on my willingness to see and understand that there *was* a wall. God took away the illness as a free gift, not because I'm being a good little mother, but because God loves Nan. How about that!

Hurdles to Happiness

by Julie Harris[*]

My first hurdle after marriage was learning to be *part* of something, not "the whole cheese." In various ways, God showed me that I had to give up the right to myself — trying to be someone on my own — and to build a new

---
[*]Wife of the Editor Emeritus, *Faith at Work* Magazine.

Children: Complication or Compensation? / 133

life "together." Two strands in a rope are stronger than one lone string!

Specifically, I had to stop thinking my job outside the home was more important than my husband's, and to "build into" his work. Like the pilings that hold up a pier, I could support my husband. I started by being interested in what was interesting to him. Along the way I even became a baseball fan.

I think God means a husband and wife to complement, not compete with, each other. It's easy for the wife to grab the family leadership in this country (we're almost a matriarchy, anyway), but how could my husband grow to be head of the household if I acted as if he were my son?

We soon found we were miserable if something came between us, so we had to keep the channels of communication open. Before we were married we had told each other all the things we were ashamed of. My husband had been specific, I more general. After about a year he asked me for the details I was ashamed of. It was painful, but it helped to unify us. There were no secret places — no hidden areas. We were indeed "one." We have tried to keep it that way ever since.

Every day we'd pray to find the will of God, for that day and for our lives. Our married daughter puts it this way: "God becomes the point of reference. It's not *who's* right, but *what's* right in making decisions."

The next most important thing, after putting God first, was to love my husband as he was. No, he wasn't perfect. Neither was I. My job was to love him, not reform him. And he didn't seem to have so many faults, after all, when I let God deal with *my* resentments and hurt feelings. In every situation there was one factor that could be changed — *me*. Often that was enough.

When the children came (we have three), we wanted them to know God as a living force in their lives. We hoped we'd have such a wonderful atmosphere in our home that they would naturally grow into a vital faith. It didn't work that way. They each had or still have to decide for themselves. When they do, there's no joy like it for the old folks at home!

However, I believe we did provide a background against which the children could make decisions. We started with "thank you" prayers at bedtime. These were spontaneous, mostly recalling the good things that had happened during the day, and thanking God for them. The children were encouraged to add their own ideas. It's so difficult for many grown-ups to pray aloud that it's good to start naturally and simply when the children are small.

Sometimes we'd add a "sorry" prayer for something done wrong, but we didn't want God to be associated with punishment. It helped immeasurably if Mother or Dad asked forgiveness for something *they* had done wrong.

And there was no substitute for our own faith. If it weren't real to us, it wouldn't be real to the children.

As they grew older we tried a corporate time of prayer. We called it "family council ring." Just to add color, we all sat on the floor in a circle, like Indians, sometimes swathed in blankets to make it more dramatic.

We tried to do this once a week, adding a time of listening to the vocalized prayers. The telephone provided a good example to make this real to the children: no one would think of telephoning and hanging up before getting a reply. If God could hear us, He could get His thoughts through to us.

Finally, just to keep the "council ring" fun, we would

Children: Complication or Compensation? / 135

end with a cheery time which varied from story-telling to "rough-house."

Years later, our son was in a low spot. He had not been accepted at medical school, and didn't want to try another field. My husband asked if he believed in what we used to do. He said he did, and we had a time of prayer and listening with four of our family present. During this time, it occurred to our son that he should cut short his vacation and visit a certain college. There he was given a chance to enter as a special student, and he is now happily on his way to becoming a doctor.

Another thing we hoped was that our home would be a place where people could come to find a personal experience of Jesus Christ. Sometimes home was a cave where we'd go to lick our wounds, but we really wanted it to be a launching-pad.

Twenty-five years ago it wasn't popular in most circles to talk about Jesus Christ. There was a lot of ridicule and opposition. But we started a group in our home every Thursday night, serving coffee and inviting all manner of people. After a while it caught on. It had top priority, and we never accepted another invitation on Thursday.

I'd scramble to get through supper and get the children into bed by seven-thirty, wondering at times if it was worth all the rush. When the children were older they joined us, and we'd all play games for half an hour.

Lasting friendships were formed on those Thursday evenings, and eventually plans were hatched for monthly meetings where we could speak publicly of our discoveries, and encourage others to try fellowship groups themselves. Later, we undertook bigger things, such as weekend conferences.

With all this activity, there couldn't help but be tensions between home and outside work. I felt I wouldn't have much of a "witness" if my children were running wild, so I tried first to make sure they were taken care of — but there were exceptions. One night I was supposed to attend a meeting, and a child was in tears because she didn't understand her homework. I was torn between two loyalties. That time I went to the meeting, reminding the little girl that God had helped me and would help her, too. On returning home, I found a note pinned to my pillow: "I did as you said, and He helped. I understood perfectly." If I had stayed at home she would have missed the experience of finding God able.

When our children went away to college, we'd look forward eagerly to their return for vacations. I'd cook their favorite foods, and we would anticipate a wonderful time of hearing all about everything. It never happened that way. After dinner they would evaporate — to the telephone, to their rooms, and out for the evening. My husband and I would swallow our disappointment and try not to show it. If we could be patient, they always came back, usually about midnight two nights later, and would sit at the foot of the bed and pour out all the news we had hoped to hear. What did lack of sleep matter if we were close to our children again!

We are now entering the less active years, and find it takes much more strength to do what we loved to do before. What was easy then is now an effort. Will old age bring bitter complaining or a chance to show courage and faith? With more enforced leisure there is more time for prayer, listening to people, seeing needs.

My husband and I were very fortunate to begin our marriage "under God's direction." We felt He wanted us to form a new unit of society because we would be more useful to Him that way.

Children: Complication or Compensation?

The eternal triangle should feature in every marriage, only instead of "the other woman" substitute God at the apex. You and your mate are at the base angles. Then, as you draw nearer to God, you draw nearer to each other.

How Young Is Too Young?

Emotionally, Billy's mother wanted him to depend only on her for his security, but this attitude didn't jibe with the way of life she had discovered for herself.

Temper, stubbornness, childish fears, disobedience — every child has his share. Modern parents talk glibly about "behavior problems." Old-fashioned parents depended on a razor strop or hairbrush to correct the small criminal. What approach should a Christian parent take? I am the mother of an active, runabout boy, and I have asked myself this question many, many times. More important, I have asked God. And the answer? One that startles me.

"Pray with Billy. Pray for him. Teach him to pray."

Billy is only two and a half years old. My intellect and an assortment of psychology books tend to reject the idea that prayer can have any real meaning for a youngster of that age. I would prefer not to believe that Christ is as adequate for my child's sins as for mine, and in the same way. Secretly, I would like Billy to be brave because *I* reassure him, to obey because *I* say so. I'd like him to depend on me for all his security, rather than on Christ. God has to show me again and again that this is just plain possessiveness, and very wrong.

We have been teaching Billy to pray for nearly two years. Besides using a formal prayer at meals and bedtime, we have tried to make prayer a natural, spontaneous part of daily life. I think it is natural for a child to love and pray to Jesus. There are pictures to look at and stories to tell to create a feeling of personal friendship with our Lord.

A little child's prayers are of several kinds. Roughly I classify them as: "thank you" prayers; "help me" prayers; "tell me" prayers; and "I'm sorry" prayers.

It wasn't until recently that I realized Billy's prayers hadn't passed the "thank you" stage. That was the day we acquired a secondhand vacuum cleaner. It is an exceptionally terrifying vacuum. It roars and jumps along and tries to swallow the rug.

Billy is not ordinarily timid, but that day he nearly had hysteria. Nothing I said or did could give him the assurance and control he needed. So we said his first "help me" prayer. I held him tight, and talked about how Jesus had made Mommy and Billy (which he knew), and that Jesus had also told the man how to make the vacuum cleaner, and wouldn't let it hurt him. Then I prayed aloud that Jesus would help Billy love the vacuum cleaner.

Be prepared to have your children's prayers answered! Billy now loves that vacuum so passionately that he doesn't want me to use it unless he is helping to push.

I have such little faith that I am always surprised when prayer works. Just this morning we had a stormy and tearful hour when nothing went right. I scolded and punished and did everything but pray. Nothing stopped the whining. Finally we both sat down on the "cry-baby chair" (where people sit if they have to cry).

"Billy," I said, "do you remember how Jesus told the boat not to sink?"

"And the boat didn't sink," said Billy.

"That's right," I replied. 'The boat did what Jesus said.

Children: Complication or Compensation? / 139

Well, if Jesus says, 'Don't cry,' *then Billy won't cry*. Now you listen and see what Jesus has to say to you." We sat for a minute, then got up from the chair. After about an hour the peace and quiet began to astonish me. Billy was happily playing with a toy. Once more God has shown me He has power I do not have.

God can give Billy another quality that I cannot: repentance. Last week I had a minor rebellion on my hands. "I don't want to," was said loud and often. This ended by Billy's slapping me. Then came the final declaration of independence: "I don't want to be sorry." He sat stubbornly for a quarter hour, maintaining this attitude.

Well, I didn't think it was wise or helpful to spank him for slapping me, but frankly he had me up a tree, and knew it. I went into the next room and prayed for direction. My eye fell on a picture of the Good Shepherd, and I took it to Billy.

"See the little lamb?" I asked. "He's sorry he ran away. Let's ask Jesus to help you be sorry, too." Then I bowed my head and asked Him.

Billy took the picture and resistance melted.

"Mommy, I'm sorry now," he said. Prayer had conquered his stubborn will, and he surrendered not to his mother's will, but to God's.

One morning he was kicking the table, and I asked in exasperation, "Billy, what is it that makes you swing your feet like that?"

"Is it that old debbil?" he asked, interested at once.

"Yes, I think it must be," I answered, trying not to laugh. "How shall we get rid of him?"

"Ask Jesus," Billy said promptly. So I helped him apply his own remedy and the devil departed, as always when Jesus is mentioned.

The thing I see most clearly about these childish incidents is that each one represents a fundamental principle of Christian character: learning to pray, conquering fear, coming to repentance, listening to God's voice, depending on Jesus, recognizing sin. These concepts are not too deep, even for a very small child. We cheat our children by assuming that Christianity is too advanced for them. All too often, well-meaning parents wait until they are "old enough to understand." One has to *accept* Jesus, not understand Him. A little child will accept Him and know Him long before the age of asking questions and reasoning. Jesus can become as close and dear and real as Mommy and Daddy if He is made part of a child's life from the very beginning. If you start early enough, lengthy explanations are sidestepped, for faith is in the very fiber of the little one's character.

He does not question what he has known since babyhood. The beginnings of character are firmly established by the age of three. It is fundamentally the business of parents, not the Sunday school. And parents will find, as I have, that Christ is the answer to a child's daily problems as well as an adult's.

Time for a Round-Table

Mom, Dad, and the three children try honesty as a means of dealing with family conflicts and irritations. It isn't always easy on the ego. . . .

My husband and I were beset by many problems which we thought were material ones, but which turned out to be fundamentally spiritual. Five years ago we were told of a way of life that really worked. We tried it, and it *did*.

Children: Complication or Compensation? / 141

By "unconditional surrender" to Christ; by seeking God's will for us; by praying for direction in carrying out His plan for us; by facing our dispositional shortcomings; we found a new basis for home life. It has never failed (unless we failed to apply it) in any subsequent problem or emergency, and we believe it has made our home into a "growing" place — and our daily work and contacts more worthwhile.

One of our experiments will illustrate what I mean:

Father: Listen to those kids quarrelling! Don't you think we'd better have a Round-Table to clear the atmosphere?

Mother: Yes, let's. I'll call them.

The children (aged nine to eleven) come in, somewhat resentfully. There are clear signs of the recent storm. To make it realistic we actually sit around the dining-room table (sometimes with paper and pencils, but not always). This time we ask them to say honestly what is on their minds, and after a pause:

Father: Robert, have you anything to tell us now?

Robert: Jennifer is a cry-baby and bawls loudest when Mother is near.

Father: Jennifer, your turn.

Jennifer: Well, Robert is bossy, and hurts my feelings when he talks like that.

Father: And now Jeannie.

Jeannie: Robert doesn't even answer when I speak to him.

Father: Is there anything on your mind, Mother?

Mother: Yes, there is. You hurt my feelings when you threw those shirts into the wastebasket last week! But how about you?

Father: It seemed to me you were being a bit of a dictator, and I took it out on the shirts.

Mother: Now that we've said what we think, let's ask

God what He feels about it. Perhaps each of us may be to blame, and not the other fellow.

A short time of quiet follows, and then we each have a chance to have our say again.

Robert: I've been selfish with the girls. I'm sorry.

Jennifer: It came to me that I'm not honest when I make a fuss near Mother. I won't do it again.

Jeannie: I do tease the others sometimes, and I'm sorry.

Mother: Well, you certainly took my breath away by calling me a dictator! But I know it's true. I want to apologize right away and promise to watch my step.

Father: I feel I should grow up and be able to take a little criticism. So here's *my* apology.

With brightened faces the children start playing, and we all feel as if a load were off our minds.

The Baby Is in Good Hands

Raymond and Georgia eagerly awaited the birth of little Paul. Then came a shocking discovery, as Raymond reveals in letters to far-away friends.

Dear Stan and Florence:

The youngest member of the Claremont Methodist Church was present today in the observation nursery with his mother. Paul Stanley Warren was seven days and eleven hours old at church time. I am sure he was the most "observed" baby in the nursery.

Georgia began to have intermittent labor pains Saturday morning, October 13. By evening they were varying between seven and fourteen minutes. Carol was having a delightful time doing the "timing." She adapted the Claremont High School cheers to the occasion, trying to get

Children: Complication or Compensation? / 143

Mom down to the serious business of regular labor. We checked in at the hospital at 11:25 p.m., and Paul Stanley was born at 12:12 a.m., October 14; weight: eight pounds, twelve ounces.

At church Sunday morning we happily announced the news. When I went back to the hospital that afternoon, filled with joy and thanksgiving, whistling happily in the warm sunlight, I felt that no one could be more blessed than we. But when I greeted Georgia in her room it was apparent that she was disturbed. She asked me to close the door, and with her heart breaking told me that Paul was Mongoloid.

Dear Stan and Florence, I hate to tell you this, to cause you to weep as we did. But we are all right now. We have been wonderfully strengthened by the love and prayers of our friends. We have felt the calming touch of Christ, and we can praise God for His goodness and mercy, and trust Him to lift us up as we surrender to Him our doubts and fears, our heartaches and anguish. We know that God reigns eternal, and believe that He will give us the strength to love Paul into the very finest boy possible.

The most terrible thought was, *How can we tell the children?* and *How can we tell our friends?* We had a strong impulse to phone you Sunday night, we were so desperately in need. But now we are glad we didn't, because it would have been only a terrible sadness that we could have shared with you. Now we can temper our sadness with the wonder of God's love, and the love of the other children for little Paul.

Sunday afternoon the obstetrician told me he was suspicious of Paul's condition but didn't want to say anything without the advice of a pediatrician. This poor man then had the job of telling Georgia the bad news. He agreed to meet me on Wednesday morning when he would examine Paul again and tell us more definitely what we could expect. He suggested the possibility of a "home," which was very disturbing to both of us.

I had to talk to someone, so I stopped in to see my mother. It was difficult to come home to the children and to answer their questions about "How's Paul?" Finally I simply told them and others that he was "in good hands."

On Wednesday we were told that the degree of mental and physical deficiency couldn't be determined, but that there is always some. The baby's general lack of muscle tone was apparent. The trained eye could detect the round face and slightly upturned eyes. We were told that he would do the things that a normal baby would do, but that his development would be slower. Unlike many Mongol babies he has a strong heart.

We brought Paul home on Thursday, and waited, wondering, as each child came home from school. How lovingly they examined their little brother, and their love grew as they took turns feeding him. He needed assistance at first, but quickly learned the trick. We think he will make the U. S. "burping" team!

After the children were all well acquainted with Paul, Georgia told Jeannette at bedtime that he would be a little slower than most babies, and would need extra care and help. With the older three we were more explicit, telling them what the doctors had told us. Tim and Chet went to bed rather quickly — all tired out. Carol went into the living room. Georgia found her crying and we tried to comfort her. We wondered what would happen the next day.

After school Carol came home, washed her hands, and picked up "her baby." She carried him all over the house until Jeannette came home and held out hungry arms. The

Children: Complication or Compensation? / 145

boys enjoy feeding Paul, and have had their friends in to look at him. We know he will be the most loved child we have ever known.

This event has already done something for us which I pray we will not lose. We take time, now, to listen to what the children say to us. We are learning patience and love in a new way. We know that life will not pass this way again, so we must look carefully at all of God's wonders around us.

Please, Stan and Florence, support us in our prayers that the Holy Spirit will give us strength and gentleness, patience and courage, love and understanding, humility, surrender of self constantly in prayer — praising God for His mercy and goodness.

We wish that you were with us.

— Raymond

o o o

. . . Paul is acting just like most normal babies. He cries lustily and lifts his head and kicks his legs hard. Our family doctor tells us he is withholding judgment until Paul is about three months old. He admits to indications of Mongolism, but feels there is some doubt.

We are sure that if prayers and love can change Paul's condition, it will be changed. . . .

o o o

. . . When Paul was examined by our family doctor at one month, we were told that an opacity was forming in his eyes which could probably develop into cataracts. The circumference of his head was also below normal for his age — another symptom of Mongolism.

This was so hard — the thought of his having to be blind along with his other problems. During the wee hours about two weeks later as I was feeding Paul, I held him lovingly in my arms, looking deep into his eyes, praying for God's healing: not words, but intense feeling and total commitment of those little eyes to God.

Then came the most positive answer to prayer that one could experience: "His eyes are all right. Don't worry any more."

Two weeks later when the doctor again examined the baby I stood waiting, without anxiety. The doctor looked puzzled. Then he said, "The opacity seems to be going away." What is more, Paul's head measurement was now in the normal range.

At three months his eyes were fine, and his height and weight on the high side of normal. X-ray studies of his hips and hands revealed normal bone structure (abnormalities of hips and little fingers at about three months can be sure indications of Mongolism).

Now the only thing medically wrong with Paul is some lack of muscle tone. We are waiting prayerfully to see what other wonders God will perform. We know we don't merit any of these blessings, but we do praise God for His love for Paul and for all of us. . . .

Epilogue

EPILOGUE

Family Life and Faith

by Horace Churchman Lukens[*]

As a pastor I am constantly called upon to help ease tensions between husbands and wives, parents and children. In a society where people are often treated as pawns, they need to be treated as persons. This means that someone must take time to listen to them.

In my youth when there were times of family tension, my father would restrain his six boisterous children by saying, "Hold your tongue!" I have had ample opportunity to put his admonition into practice as I have seen people's need to be listened to unhurriedly, to unburden themselves to someone who neither judges them, talks down to them, nor blabs their confidences. A person may not be able to open up with the deeper, more unconscious things that need to be expressed, if he feels rushed.

Nearly every day a pastor is called upon to help straighten out tangled family problems, misunderstandings between youth and age, tensions between husbands and wives. The Church is often criticized for not being involved in the life of the world; I would say that at its best the Church is very much involved as a stabilizing, unifying factor in great numbers of homes. It is gratifying to help a young couple get "over the humps" when they have run into real difficulty, and then to watch them go on to many years of an

---

[*]Minister, The Presbyterian Church, Vienna, Virginia.

increasingly strong relationship, with a useful life and happy children.

A couple asked me to come to their home. It was a long and stormy evening, going on until two o'clock in the morning. The session was violent, with tempers blazing and accusations hurled back and forth. The couple were determined to separate, convinced that their marriage was a failure. For years they had tried to make a go of it, but now it seemed hopeless. In spite of the fact that they had three young children, they could not face the future together.

They said they were incompatible; they could not trust each other; they were always fighting; their families were mixed up in it, taking sides. Still, the fact that they had called on me indicated that there was hope, and I saw their display of temper as a part of their healing. Each one needed to explode in order to be honest with himself and with his partner, and get rid of pent-up feelings of hurt and resentment.

When they finally began to see that there could be forgiveness, that they could feel differently, and that God had a purpose for them together, they calmed down and were united in a new devotion. The five hours of turmoil were well spent, for that husband and wife have been thriving together for ten years since. Blow-ups are preferable to pent-ups.

A person often wants an objective ear, not too personal, to hear him out. There is a crying need for individuals who can help others one at a time, and who have the ability to get beneath the surface to the real trouble. For those of us who call ourselves Christians, the main business of life is relating individuals to Jesus Christ. If we excuse ourselves by saying it is "too private, too sacred," or simply

Family Life and Faith / 151

that we don't know how, we will miss the opportunity to help another person to find power and victory.

"I'm in trouble," the timid little voice came over the telephone. I did not know the young girl who appeared later for the appointment. "Isn't it awful?" she said. "What's awful?" I asked. "The guilt."

She had been living with someone for five years without being married. She did not believe she could be forgiven, but when forgiveness was a reality for her, she began to straighten out her tangled life.

A conscientious man of middle years came to see me. He said he had been unfaithful to his wife years before, and a haunting sense of guilt was destroying his peace of mind and his marriage relationship. He, too, came to experience forgiveness, and then he was able to establish a new family relationship. There was a new lilt and freedom about his whole life.

If the difficulty is not marital, it may involve sickness, death, grief, crime, or any of a number of agonizing problems. If we avoid it or merely moralize about it, we are of no use whatever. If we are perceptive, know how to listen, refuse to take sides, and can point to the reality of Christ's forgiveness, helping the person to come to the point of decision-making, we may serve in a healing capacity.

One husband and wife, well along in years, were having a battle of words and nerves. Doubtless they were both difficult to live with. He was stubborn. She was overworked, her patience was exhausted, and she shouted, "I hate you!"

She had to be honest about her feelings in the presence of another person who would accept her and her "hatred." Having let the worst come out, she could be free of it; free to let the best come out. "But down underneath, you love him, don't you?" I asked.

When someone else saw her best self, she believed it was there and that it could be in control again. Years later, after her husband's death, she said to me, "We can wallow in self-pity and jealousy, but it is only as we forget ourselves and console others that we are consoled."

In his book, *Mental Health Through Christian Community* (Abingdon Press, 1965), Howard J. Clinebell, Jr., speaks of preparation for marriage and suggests that emotional immaturity is the cause of most marriage failure. "If young people knew themselves better, they would be less pushed by neurotic needs in their choices of 'roommates for life.'" Pointing out that the husband-wife relationship is vital to the emotional health of the child, he says, "Emotional illness and health tend to be transmitted from one generation to the next. . . . The health of the families of the next generation is already being deeply influenced by the experiences of children in present-day homes." "Since the child's personality growth is inextricably bound up with his parents' relationship with each other, it is imperative that that relationship be as strong and well-nourished as possible." Clinebell is speaking directly to the needs of parents when he indicates that a frustrated relationship of husband and wife makes them "unable to satisfy" the needs of their child for love, understanding, and acceptance. He adds that the old saying that "the most important thing a father can do for his child is to love the child's mother (and vice versa) contains an inescapable truth."

When Lettie Witherspoon and I were married in 1940, we had been helped by a faithful and loving Christian fellowship to face and surrender to Christ our selfish motives,

Family Life and Faith / 153

and to get our relationship Christ-centered so that He could work through us. When our two children were born, we never doubted that they were God-given. Perhaps our sharing this conviction with them as they reached the age of understanding had some part in their knowing a sense of identity, dignity, and assurance.

My wife and I were given a released love for each other, making it natural to include our children in this atmosphere. To be sure, we failed them in many ways. I personally failed them more often when they were teenagers than earlier. Yet we were able to share with them, as they grew, something of what Christ meant to us, and I am convinced that as a consequence we were spared many of the crises that characteristically disrupt the lives of families.

Many parents tear their hair over their children, wondering how to get through the "difficult years." And many youngsters tear their hair over their parents, wondering why they are so "dumb." It seems that many parents have given up the idea of family worship. By and large, the family altar has gone down the drain, with a resultant lack of depth in family life. Parents wonder whether it is worth the effort to have a "quiet time," and whether it can mean anything to their children.

When our children were young, the family quiet time meant a great deal to us. Now that they have reached adulthood, I have asked them to comment on their reactions to this emphasis. Horace, Jr., twenty-four years old as I write this, is married and doing graduate work toward his Ph.D. in clinical psychology. He writes:

"My earliest recollections of family life bring back a feeling of closeness and unity which I consider unique. This uniqueness emanates from the central place of God in all our family activities; moreover, it is attributable in part to our daily quiet times. These moments provided an opportunity for discussion and decision of family affairs in addition to a sharing of thoughts through Scripture reading and prayer. As we carried out our daily chores, this framework, in which Christ was the focal point, held a place of prominence, and guided each of us in our attitudes and relations with other people.

"Acceptance of such a Christ-oriented life was remarkably easy in light of our unceasing exposure to, and involvement in, this point of view. The fulfilling of Christian attitudes and behavior was more the rule than the exception. . . . the assurance of Christian guidance, security, and warmth never waned despite numerous physical separations between family members.

"[I am convinced] that a wholesome and firm family constellation, guided by Christ, is a prerequisite for meaningful mental and spiritual health and peace of mind."

Youngsters need the inner sense of confidence and purpose which these words imply. How are they to get it, if they do not get it in those early years from both father and mother? Yet how are parents to find it themselves unless someone helps them? We cannot help our children to find a vital relationship with Christ unless we have done so ourselves.

Dr. Clinebell, in his book quoted above, talks about couples seeking complete psychological union in marriage, and we might add "spiritual union." He says that when this is approximated ,"A new identity emerges. This new . . . identity is not simply the sum of their two personalities . . . It is a new creation resulting from the ways each unique personality interacts with the other. A good marriage relationship has dimensions of health and strength which neither could possess alone."

Family Life and Faith / 155

Our daughter Nancy, twenty-one years old and a senior in college as this is written, reports:

"I will never forget the scenes that grew out of our after-supper family prayers, when we as nine- or ten-year-olds would be called upon to plan an evening's devotions, which would include reciting or reading Bible selections, singing, praying, and sharing thoughts together. Too often on hot summer evenings our thoughts escaped to the baseball game scheduled with the kids next door; but a sudden, 'What came to you, Nancy?' would remind me that at the moment prayer was more important.

"As a child I was often surprised at the way my parents responded to situations in which I should have expected punishment. I remember being spanked only once — I have no idea what for. Most of the time the emphasis was on my finding out for myself what was wrong about what I had done, and being sorry for it. In decision-making I was seldom told what to do, but left to decide for myself and to sense what my parents thought of the situation.

"Not until last summer did I understand this approach. In the meantime I had grown further and further away from home while growing into new ideas and situations at college, and more and more convinced that my parents would never understand me. I was almost dreading a summer at home alone with my parents when final exams were over in May. Then, at a Faith at Work conference, God healed the widening gap in my relationship with my parents. I had gone to a workshop on 'Creative Relationships' where someone mentioned Horace Lukens' definition of Christian love: 'Wanting God's best for someone and living so he can find it.'

"Hearing my father's name startled me at first more than the definition; I'm sure no one there knew that Horace

Lukens' daughter was on the scene, desperately looking for an answer to a problem. But what struck me most was that this thought had been operative in our household and in my father's ministry for years, and yet I had to come here to discover it and accept it.

"After a good talk together, our family found God in a new way, as I have been doing again and again ever since. I hope that when I have a family we will let God run our home as my parents have succeeded in doing."

A young person needs to be helped to see what goes into a decision, what it means in daily life, and how to make it. A sixteen-year-old girl said to me that she did not feel ready to make a decision to let Christ have her life. I agreed that she was not ready at that moment to make a thoroughgoing decision, but suggested that she could make *some* decision, and asked if she would be willing to ask God to make her *willing* to give herself to Him. She wanted to do this. Immediately she was freer, happier, more relaxed, able to think straight about boys, and saying, "Now the Bible and church make sense!"

When we try to help people, we are sometimes overwhelmed with a sense of the power of evil and hate. But the longer I live, the more I am convinced that the power of love wins out over the power of hate and resentment. Every day I witness the power of forgiveness to heal the human heart; the power of God's divine, redemptive love in and through Jesus Christ to heal broken relationships and remake human nature.

Paul Tournier suggests in one of his fascinating books that real love in marriage is an experience of grace, for in it we know that, like all the best gifts, we do not deserve it. This should give us a clue to the glorious Gospel of God's grace, and our share in it, when we know that of ourselves we are

Family Life and Faith / 157

hopelessly lost, vain and empty, but that through the grace of God in Jesus Christ we may receive life.

The more I know of people the more firmly I am convinced that it is only when two persons first surrender themselves to God and experience His love individually and separately that they are able to love one another and surrender themselves to each other in true devotion. Only as we relinquish our self-will to God can we give ourselves to another person in any way other than a projection of our self on him.

This is perhaps the meaning of the symbolism in the marriage ceremony when, in response to the question, "Who giveth this woman to be married to this man?" the bride's father places her hand in the hand of the minister, who stands as the representative of Christ. Only as she is given to Christ is she ready for marriage.

I believe that all our experiments in interpersonal relationships lead inevitably to a theological relationship: God-and-thou, God-and-me; I-and-thou. It seems that God has so designed human nature that we fail when we leave Him out. We are always less than we can be, when He is not in the picture. I am sure that all the forms of humanistic, man-made, horizontal relationships ultimately leave us empty. But when we open up our motives and our wills to God, we can receive a gift of love from Him which He is constantly offering to us.